Recipes to the Rescue 2

Stray Rescue
of **Saint Louis**

Recipes to the Rescue 2

A Salute to the Stray Rescue Community

Stray Rescue of St. Louis
2320 Pine St.
St. Louis, MO 63103

314.771.6121

DEDICATED TO

Randy Grim, staff and volunteers of Stray Rescue St. Louis

Cover artwork donated by Dean Russo Art
http://www.deanrussoart.bigcartel.com

First Edition 2015
Published by Stray Rescue St. Louis
2320 Pine St., St Louis, MO 63103
314.771.6121
314.781.0001

© Copyright 2015 Stray Rescue of St. Louis

ISBN-978-0-692-49233-8
Designed by Cathy Wood Book Design
Email: woodce@swbell.net

Printed in the United States of America

Mission and History of Stray Rescue of St. Louis

I am often asked how I started Stray Rescue of St. Louis. I ask myself that, too. I never devised a game plan or had a vision; I guess it was born out of necessity. I hated my job as a flight attendant. I figured there had to be more to life than saying, "chicken or beef." Little did I know that this career move would one day evolve into two no-kill shelters with a hundreds of volunteers, and have an impact on the stray dog crisis in America. I love the dogs I save. I feel their pain, so I keep up the act of "Dog Man" or, as a homeless man calls me, "Coyote Man," so those canines don't suffer and die. That's pretty much why I became the founder of Stray Rescue.

I suffer from social anxiety. I have some phobias. I am gay. I am a shy, private kind of guy—by no means a hero. I have been thrust into the dog limelight from a previous book about my work. It forces me to try to be more outgoing and confident. You know, exude that Rambo-type of confidence.

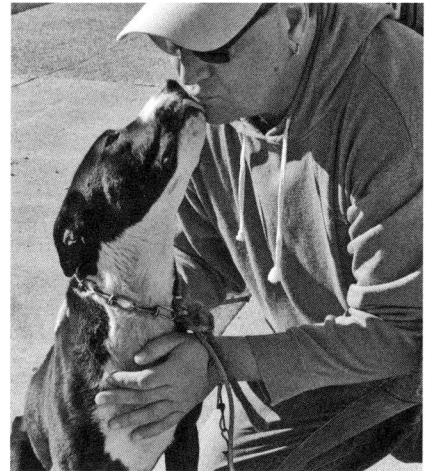
Randy Grim and with his pal Jimmy K

In 1990 I learned the fine art of cutting dog hair. It's not something I really wanted to do, but I thought it would at least point me in the direction of my dream of working with animals. I'd see stray dogs—some in packs—pass by the Lafayette Square grooming shop where I worked. In an effort to get them off the streets, I'd make the normal calls to the local shelters and government agencies, only to find out that these dogs simply are out of luck. I started to think of ways to catch them, and before long I invented some wacky capture methods. I also enlisted friends to help save these poor guys. Each year, this makeshift organization grew as I overloaded everyone I knew with a stray dog.

Stray Rescue officially was born in 1998 as a full-fledged non-profit organization and shelter. I still have no idea how I did it, except that I had no choice. These generous people take in sickly, traumatized animals and, with time and the support of professional animal trainers and behaviorists, give back healthy, loving companions ready for adoption. Stray Rescue's foster network is the largest and most effective program of its kind in the St. Louis area. Stray Rescue has made a significant impact and become a voice for stray animals everywhere. With fabulous volunteers, veterinarians, trainers, behaviorists, shelters and programs, I continue to be amazed at how this organization has evolved. But there is so much more work to do because these poor animals continue to suffer. Some days it feels as if I'm fighting a never-ending battle, but it's a battle that I must wage—for their sake.

Stray Rescue's mission is to lead the way towards making St. Louis a compassionate city where every companion animal knows health, comfort, and affection, and no stray is euthanized merely because he or she has been abandoned, abused, or neglected. As part of our mission, Stray Rescue is out on the streets daily taking a progressive, proactive approach to establishing a permanent resolution to the stray companion animal problem through dedicated rescue efforts, sheltering, community outreach programs, education, collaborations, and the encouragement of responsible pet guardianship.

Virtually all of the pets we save have been abused and neglected. They've been dumped on highways, or remote country roads. Abandoned in public parks, empty houses and dark alleys. We've even saved dogs left chained behind buildings after their owners had moved away.

Rescued animals often make the best pets. Pets from Stray Rescue seem to understand that they have a second lease on life. In return for a little affection and attention, these remarkable animals reward their new owners with a love and loyalty unmatched anywhere.

– Randy Grim, Founder and Director of Stray Rescue of St. Louis

Animal Cruelty Task Force

In 2012, Stray Rescue founded the Animal Cruelty Task Force in partnership with St. Louis City Mayor Francis Slay, St. Louis City Chief of Police and Director of the Health Department along with two police officers dedicated to finding the abusers and bringing them to justice. We are currently making case law by changing mere misdemeanors to felonies that carry up to four years in prison. When abusers receive citations, they are required to come to Stray Rescue to participate in a Responsible Pet Guardianship Class. The Animal Cruelty Task Force notes a groundbreaking partnership with key St. Louis agencies, and it's a leading national example of how a multi-agency alliance can drastically improve the landscape for all companion animals. There have been many successful convictions since the inception of the program.

Stray Rescue – Uno

Ways to Help

Saving Pets & Enriching Lives through Dierberg's Markets. Stray Rescue of St. Louis helps save abandoned pets from disease, neglect and death on the streets. Make a donation to Stray Rescue at any Dierbergs checkout! Just tell your cashier the amount you wish to donate. You will receive a receipt with the amount donated for your records. 100% of your donation goes directly to Stray Rescue.

BRICK BY BRICK BUILDING A SHELTER ONE MEMORY AT A TIME

All the proceeds from these memorial bricks go towards the construction of our main adoption and dog apartment area; a space that will be incredibly enriching and comfortable for dogs. And believe it or not, we care about people too! We want them to know the joy a shelter dog brings. With this area completed, it'll be easier to find the perfect companion, leading to more adoptions and highlighting the human-dog bond. This phase of shelter renovations will consist of replacing existing temporary kennels with 20 extraordinary dog apartments, as well as a laundry room, kitchen, and shelter manager's office.

THE Stracks Fund

Donate via our website to support our emergency medical care fund. Many of the dogs that are rescued have life threatening medical issues and often need emergency care. The Stracks fund is dedicated to help pay for the needed veterinary care.

Our Wishlist

If you would like to help us in our efforts to save homeless animals, the following is a list of items we use most often. Stray Rescue of St. Louis depends on the generous donations received by the public. We thank you from the bottom of our hearts!

- Pop-Top Canned Dog Food
- Blankets & Towels (gently used)
- Bleach & Cleaning Supplies
- Braunschweiger, Cheese Whiz®, Peanut Butter, & Hot Dogs
- Martingale/No Slip® Dog Collars (Medium & Large Size)
- Cat Toys
- Kong® Toys
- Nylabones®
- Surgical Gloves
- Large Wire Crates (36" – 52")
- Cat & Dog Treats
- Dog Harnesses (Medium & Large Size)
- Cat & Dog Beds, collars & leashes
- Liquid Fabric Softener & Dye-Free Laundry Detergent
- Paper Towels & Toilet Paper
- Garbage Bags (55 Gallon & 13 Gallon)
- Litter & Litter Boxes
- OdoBan®, Lysol®, or other Air Sanitizers

Online Store: Now you can order Stray Rescue merchandise from the comfort of your own home! Your purchase has a direct impact on providing care for our beloved homeless companion animals—thank you for your support! Shipping is available. **www.Strayrescue.org**

Volunteer Opportunities

At Stray Rescue, we're always looking for dedicated volunteers! We couldn't survive without them. To volunteer, fill out our online volunteer form at strayrescue.org, or call us at 314-771-6121. New Volunteer orientations are held throughout the week. Your help is greatly appreciated! Some of the events and activities that we can always use help for are as follows:

- People to care for and walk animals staying at our 2 shelters in St. Louis City, even if it is one hour a week or everyday.
- People to help lead adoption events, or handle shelter dogs/cats at adoption events.
- Recruitment of committed volunteers and fosters.
- People to work with fundraising and fundraising events.
- Help with information booths and merchandise tables at special events.
- Volunteers for Stray Rescue events (Urban Wanderers, Holiday Gala, Golf Tournament, etc)

BECOMING A STRAY RESCUE FOSTER PARENT is one of the most helpful, heartfelt things you could possibly do for a homeless companion animal. As a foster, you provide a temporary loving home for an abandoned dog or cat until he or she finds a forever home. Many of those we rescue have lived difficult lives on harsh city streets, and fosters are essential to showing these animals what it means to trust, feel safe, and experience comfort. Whether your foster is with you for several days or several months, the knowledge that you helped immensely will last a lifetime

STRAY RESCUE REHABILITATION ENRICHMENT PROGRAM (REP): This program has been designed for volunteers that seek to take extra steps in the rehabilitation process of a particular dog. We are aware that certain bonds form between individuals and select dogs, and that these relationships are highly valuable to the dogs during their time within our shelter. By participating in the R.E.P., you are committing to the mental and physical wellbeing of this animal all the way up until the point of adoption.

PUPPIES FOR PAROLE – Stray Rescue dogs are paired with offenders at a medium-security correctional center for a three month period. Benefiting both the offenders and the dogs with which they are paired, Puppies For Parole allows for consistent socialization and training of rescued shelter dogs with the goal of each dog obtaining their Canine Good Citizen (CGC) certification and increasing their chances of being adopted by the end of the program. The offenders benefit by feeling a sense of accomplishment and giving back to the community.

Stray Rescue – Josephine

⋈ Sponsor ⋈

Karen O'dell – In memory of Max O'Dell

⋈ Patron ⋈

Karen Groesser

James R. and Karen S. Freebersyser

Peggy Oates

Mary Kay Candido and John Elser

Ken Kleiman

Caitlin Deneau

Michael and Dawn Harrod

Lisa Campbell – In Honor and Memory of all my Black Cats. Bart, Hazel, Merlyn and TessaMae

Ashlee Long

Marci Kelley

Greg & Rosie Corcoran

Martha and John Adamson

Cheryl Linneman

⋈ Rescuer ⋈

Heidi and Jon Greene

Margie Redenbaugh

Lucy and Reid Bloomstran – in honor of Chloe, Beau and all the dogs at 18th Street"

Shirley Dockens

⋈ Guardian ⋈

The Whiteaker Family

Ellen Morgan, LLC

John Ard

The Deneau Family

Helping Hands for Furry Friends

Amy Schuster

Jan Blomefield In Honor of the 18th Street Volunteers

Susan Toretta – In memory of Kyle Toretta. Love Mom and Dad

Connie Hall – In memory of Judy, Midnight, Smokey and Cotton

Dedication

As a volunteer with Stray Rescue of St. Louis, I have witnessed firsthand the role community plays in this organization. It begins with the community of staff who are some of the hardest working, dedicated people I know. I am one of hundreds of volunteers. There are people that give their time to take care of the shelter pets and teach them what it is to love, trust, and get them ready for their forever homes. There are enrichment team members that spend time socializing the shelter dogs and extend the time spent learning how to be a family pet, and no longer have to survive on their own. There are families that open their homes to foster the pets, and teach them how to live in a home, with a family, other pets, so when they are adopted, the transition will be easier for them. Lastly, there are the adopters, the forever guardians who allow the rescue pets to rescue them.

On a larger scale, the community of St. Louis provides invaluable support. The businesses, restaurants, and universities that contribute volunteers, donations, and fund raising events, to the involvement of our professional sports teams. St. Louis is a very charitable town that cares about animals.

Special thanks go to my friend Jenn Foster. Jenn's compassion for people is only surpassed by her compassion for animals. She was instrumental in guiding the success of the first Recipes to the Rescue, and building on the success of that cookbook, asked me to do another one. I couldn't say no. I am grateful for her knowledge and support. I am grateful for her ability to provide calm and perspective during the times I was not able to see it. I am blessed to call you friend.

Special thanks to Caryn Dugan (Stlveggiegirl) for helping to identify and label all vegetarian recipes. In addition to volunteering her time, she was also a great supporter of both cookbooks as a contributor and a sponsor.

Photo Dedication Collage Design Tony Marshall Photos provided by Lisa Campbell, Liz McKibben, Nikole Ventimiglia, Scott Daum, Sandy Minor. Other photos throughout the book were provided by countless volunteers and staff that care for the shelter pets on a daily basis.

Kissing booth photos on dividers and back cover are credited to Lynn Terry Photography www.lynnterry.com. In addition to being a gifted photographer, she volunteers countless hours to different shelters to provide photos of homeless pets to help them find their forever home. Our Stray Rescue pups, Oreo and Ringo are featured in these photos. Photo of Randy and Jimmy K by Donna Lochmann.

Volunteers who helped with restaurant solicitation, advertising, and social media contacts: Tessa Gauzy, Michelle Streiff, Peggy Oates, Sandy Minor, Dawn Marston, Shelly Ziemba Scopel, Mandy Martin, Gretchen Szydlowski, Jan Burton Marino, Susan Toretta, Heidi and Jon Greene, Julie McGinnis, Marcellus Gracchus, Deb Lanter, Karen Freebersyser, Pat Struckel, and Lisa Campbell. Thank you for helping spread the word. This book would not be what it is without your help.

Editing was completed by Marianne Junger and Paulette Koons. Thank you for volunteering your time to complete this task.

Last, but never least, I am grateful to my husband Brian Deneau and our daughter Caitlin for their love, support and assistance during this journey. From assembling restaurant packets, creating spreadsheets to delivering packets and soliciting recipes, you were both instrumental in getting Recipes to the Rescue 2 up and running. I am truly blessed.

Bone Appetit!
Sarah Deneau

Stray Rescue – Pask

TABLE OF CONTENTS

(V) *denotes vegetarian recipes*

Stray Rescue – Jelly Belly

Restaurant Recipes

Butternut Squash Soup (V)

EXECUTIVE CHEF BOB COLOSIMO
Eleven Eleven Mississippi

1 butternut squash, roasted, skin and seeds removed
½ white onion, peeled and roasted
⅛ tsp turmeric
1 tsp curry powder
¼ tsp cinnamon
1 Tbsp molasses
1 Tbsp ground ginger
3 C vegetable stock
⅛ C cream, optional
Salt and pepper to taste
Pinch of cayenne

In a heavy bottom sauce pan, add the butternut squash, onion, turmeric, curry powder, cinnamon, molasses, ground ginger and vegetable stock. Bring to a slow simmer and cook for 15-20 minutes. Remove from the heat and blend mixture until smooth. Return to sauce pan. Add cream and season with salt, pepper and cayenne. Simmer for 5 minutes. Taste and adjust seasonings. Serve immediately. For a slightly sweet soup, honey may be added to taste. Serves 4-6.

Dill Pickle Soup

Fountain on Locust

1½ lb bag of potatoes, cubed
2 gallons of chicken broth
28 dill pickles chopped
4 C sour cream
4 C milk

Cook potatoes in broth until soft. Add pickles and continue to cook. Puree with immersion blender. Blend milk and sour cream. Temper by adding small amounts of soup to the sour cream mixture. Slowly add sour cream mixture to soup, stirring as you go. Sprinkle with a dollop of sour cream and dried dill.

IPA Beer Chili

PW Pizza

1 lb ground beef
2 (15 oz) cans pinto beans
2 (15 oz) cans black beans
1 (14.5 oz) can diced tomatoes with peppers
1 large yellow onion, diced
2 large green peppers, diced
1 jalapeño deseeded, diced
1 tsp cocoa powder
½ pkg chili seasoning
12 oz favorite local IPA® beer
24 oz water
½ Tbsp beef base
1 C oil
Salt and pepper to taste

Sauté the peppers and onions together with oil. Add ground beef and chili seasoning to brown. Add the beer and reduce down. Once reduced, add all other ingredients, bring to a boil and simmer for 1 hour. Adjust seasoning and thicken with slurry. Serves 6. 🦴

She Crab Soup

EXECUTIVE CHEF IVY MAGRUDER
Panorama Restaurant at the St. Louis Art Museum

1 lb butter
1 C flour
1 bottle sherry
1 stalk celery (send through robo cheese grater)
3 yellow onions (send through robo cheese grater)
2 gallons shrimp stock
⅓ C Worcestershire® sauce
3 lb crab meat (claw meat)
1 qt 40% heavy cream
1 C flying fish roe
Salt and pepper to taste

In pot, melt butter with celery and onions. Whisk in flour. Deglaze with sherry, then reduce by half. Add water, base, Worcestershire and 5 cans of crab. Bring to a boil. Add cream, boil, and thicken. Turn off heat; add remaining crab and roe. 🦴

Yellow Tomato Gazpacho (V)

Scape, An American Bistro

Ingredients for presentation when serving:

1 tsp basil sorbet

3 pcs preserved lemon peel, sliced thin

2 grape tomatoes, halved

3 avocado balls, Parisienne scooped

5 pcs cucumber, peeled, seeded and dice

7 brioche croutons, olive-oil fried

¼ tsp chives, minced

Place all prepared ingredients in a chilled serving dish. Using a ladle, add 8 oz. of the gazpacho base (see recipe below) to a small wine carafe. Serve the carafe along with the chilled prepared ingredients. Add soup to the prepared ingredients.

Yellow Tomato Gazpacho Base

2 lbs yellow tomatoes, peeled, seeded and chopped

10 oz English Hot House cucumber, peeled, seeded and chopped

6 oz green onion, white part only, chopped

6 oz yellow bell pepper, chopped

7 oz water

2 oz canola oil

2 oz olive oil, extra virgin

2 oz champagne vinegar

2 oz bread crumb, from crustless baguette

1 clove garlic, peeled

Pinch of ground cumin

Pinch of Kosher salt

Place all prepared ingredients together in a stainless steel pan or bowl and refrigerate overnight. Using an immersion blender, puree. Season with salt and put back into the cooler. Serves 4.

Night of Ransom Cocktail (V)

BARTENDER MIKE
Hendel's Market Cafe

1 oz of Ransom barrel-aged gin

½ oz of Campari® Italian bitter liquor

½ oz of Luxardo® Maraschino liquor

¾ oz of Luxardo® simple syrup

¾ oz of lemon juice

Shake and strain in a snifter. Garnish with Luxardo cherries.

Poblano Chicken Chowder

Canyon Café

Roux:

1 stick unsalted butter, melted
¾ C flour

Soup Base:

1 Tbsp olive oil
½ lb onion, diced
½ lb, celery, diced
½ lb carrots, diced
¼ lb Poblano chiles, seeded and diced
1 Tbsp garlic, minced
1 tsp thyme leaves
½ Tbsp ground white pepper
1 Tbsp ground cumin
2 qt strong chicken stock (or chicken bouillon and water)
1½ Tbsp tabasco
½ bunch cilantro, washed and finely chopped
1 qt heavy cream
1 lb chicken breast, grilled and diced
Tortilla chip strips
Shredded jack cheese for topping

Make a roux by heating melted butter with flour and whisking over medium high heat for 5 minutes. Do no brown this mixture. It should be a blonde color. Heat oil in a large kettle. Add onions, carrots, poblanos and garlic. Sauté until onions become translucent and carrots begin to soften. Add thyme, pepper and cumin and stir well. Add chicken stock. Bring to a boil, reduce to simmer and cook 20 minutes or until vegetables are soft. Begin adding roux and whisk in each bit to incorporate. Be careful not to form lumps. Continue to look over high heat for 5 minutes to remove the flour taste. Remove from heat and add tabasco and cilantro. Add cream and diced chicken, then heat through. Top with crisp tortilla strips and jack cheese.

Stray Rescue – Jaelyn

Turkish Red Lentil Soup (V)

Aya Sofia Restaurant

2 Tbsp extra virgin olive oil
½ large white onion, finely diced
1 large clove garlic, minced
5 C chicken or vegetable stock
½ C red lentils
¼ C medium grain white rice
2 Tbsp tomato paste
1 tsp paprika
½ Tbsp dried mint
Cayenne pepper to taste
Salt and pepper to taste

Heat the olive oil in a large pot over high heat. Add the onion and sauté until it softens, about 2 minutes. Add the garlic and stir for another 2 minutes. Add all of the remaining ingredients; season with cayenne, salt and pepper. Bring the soup to a boil, reduce heat to medium-low and simmer until the lentils and rice are thoroughly cooked, about 30-40 minutes.

Spicy Cucumber/Yogurt Salad Dressing (V)

Blueberry Hill

2 lbs plain fat-free yogurt
1 large cucumber, peeled, seeded and pureed
4 scallions, sliced and pureed with 1/2" of green
3 Tbsp dried dill weed
1 Tbsp ground cumin
2 tsp salt
1 tsp cayenne pepper
¾ C oil (at Blueberry Hill, we use a blend of 80% canola oil and 20% olive oil)

Puree cucumbers and scallions together in food processor. Combine all ingredients except oil in mixing bowl on medium speed and blend for a few minutes. Turn mixer to slow speed and gradually add oil until dressing thickens.

Gringo's Shrimp Coctel Sauce

CHEF ROBERT MCCLELLAN
Gringo's Mexican Restaurant in the Central West End neighborhood

2 Tbsp oil
½ C white onion, diced
½ C red bell pepper, diced
2 cloves garlic, minced
1 Chipotle pepper in a can
¼ C honey
½ C red vinegar
2 C ketchup
2 Tbsp horseradish
1 C water
1 bottle Mandarina Jarrito® (orange Mexican soda)
¼ C cilantro, chopped
¼ C salt
Cooked shrimp and saltines for serving

Add the oil into pot and put on medium heat. Add onions and bell pepper, and sweat until soft (no browning.) Throw in the garlic and a pinch of salt to help bring out the moisture in the vegetables. Drizzle in the honey and cook for 5 minutes. Add the red wine vinegar and chipotle pepper and cook for another 5 minutes. Add the water, horseradish and rest of the salt, then stir to combine. Cook at a simmer for 30 minutes. Once ready, transfer to a blender and puree until smooth. Leave the sauce uncovered in the refrigerator until cold.

Right before serving, take the Jarrito and cilantro, and adjust the thickness to your liking. This brings a sweet fizzy orange flavor to the sauce. Due to the carbonation in the Jarrito, you want to be sure to only add in right before serving. Put cooked shrimp (chopped or whole) into the sauce with a side of saltines for dipping.

Diablitos Pineapple Salsa (V)

CHEF WIL PELLY
Diablitos Cantina

1 large pineapple, peeled, cored and halved
1 large yellow onion, peeled and cut into rings
1 bunch of fresh cilantro, leaves only; discard stems
1 tsp kosher salt

Grill pineapple and onion till nice dark grill marks appear, then let cool. Run a sharp knife through the cilantro a few times. Do this as quick and sharp as possible so not to bruise the herb. Dice onion and pineapple into little pieces. Mix the fruit, vegetable and herbs together and add salt.

Grab some chips and a margarita and enjoy.

Bacon Muffins

CHEF CASSY VIRES

2 slices bacon, chopped finely
2 C all-purpose flour
2¼ tsp baking powder
½ tsp salt
2 Tbsp light brown sugar
1 egg
1 C whole milk
2 Tbsp melted bacon drippings

Preheat oven to 425 degrees. Grease (or spray with cooking spray) a 12-cup muffin tin or line with paper liners. Pan fry the chopped bacon in a small, heavy saucepan until crispy. Remove with a slotted spoon and let cool slightly. In a large bowl, whisk the flour, baking powder, salt and light brown sugar together until well combined. Add bacon pieces and stir until they are well distributed and coated in the flour mixture. Lightly beat the egg in a medium bowl. Add the milk and the bacon drippings, and stir to combine. Add the milk mixture to the dry ingredients all at once, stir quickly until just combined, then stir 5-6 more times until well blended. Do not stir until smooth. Drop batter by spoonfuls into the greased muffin tin, filling each cup 2/3 full. Bake for 20 minutes or until lightly browned. Makes 12.

Edamame Dip (V)

Sub Zero Vodka Bar

1 (12 oz) frozen bag soybeans
2 whole jalapenos
1½ oz of cilantro
4 whole green onions
8 leaves of mint
Juice of 6 limes
6 oz extra virgin olive oil
¾ C cold water
Salt to taste

Flash beans in water to thaw. Blend all ingredients together in a food processor. Serve with pita bread. Deep fry pita bread, if desired.

Quick Pickled Cherry Tomatoes (V)

EXECUTIVE CHEF ZACH FLYNN
Eclipse Restaurant

1 pint cherry tomatoes, halved
¾ C white balsamic vinegar
1 Tbsp kosher salt
2½ Tbsp granulated fine sugar
1 sprig of thyme
¼ Tbsp coriander seed

Bring vinegar, sugar, salt, thyme and coriander to a simmer. Remove from heat and let cool to about 90 degrees. Pour liquid over tomatoes and cool overnight. Makes 1 pint pickled tomatoes. Serve over arugala.

Molasses Vinaigrette

3 Tbsp dark balsamic vinegar
¾ Tbsp molasses
¾ Tbsp honey
1 dash of salt
¾ C blended oil

Blend, or whisk vigorously, vinegar, molasses, honey and salt. While blending, slowly add oil to emulsify. Makes about 1 cup of dressing. 🦴

BBQ Oysters

CHEF REX HALE
360

4 oz extra virgin olive oil
8 oz unsalted butter
3 Tbsp garlic, minced
1 large shallot, minced
½ tsp red pepper flake
1 tsp smoked sea salt
2 oz red bell pepper, minced
2 oz parsley, finely chopped
2 lemons cut into wedges without pith or seed
16 large oysters (Blue Point Delaware or similar)

Cook garlic, shallots, salt, pepper flake and bell pepper in olive oil. Cool slightly. Meanwhile, whip butter in an electric mixer until it doubles in volume. Add the oil and vegetable mixture to the butter on a low speed; add parsley. Spoon mixture over oysters and bake at 500 degrees until browned slightly. Serve on sea salt-lined plates and garnish with a lemon wedges. Serves 4. 🦴

Ahi Tuna Thin and Raw

CHEF REX HALE
The Restaurant at the Cheshire

10 oz skinless Ahi Tuna, blood line removed, very thinly sliced
2 medium heirloom tomatoes, peeled, seeded, cut into sixteenth wedges and cut in half
½ large Fresno chile, seeded, rib removed and finely diced
6 pitted Cuquillo olives (or Nicoise olives), finely diced
20 baby arugula leaves
Juice of half of a Lime
4 tsp high quality extra virgin olive oil
2 tsp high quality grated Parmesan cheese
Coarse sea salt and freshly ground black pepper, to taste
Micro cilantro for garnish
Heirloom tomatoes cut into wedges for garnish

Place 2½ ounces of the thinly sliced Ahi Tuna on the plate top with equal amount of tomato wedges, minced Fresno chile and minced olives. Garnish each plate with arugula leaves drizzle with equal amounts of lime juice and extra virgin olive oil. Season the fish to taste with coarse sea salt and freshly ground black pepper. Sprinkle equally with grated Parmesan and top with micro cilantro. Serve with wafer-thin crostini prepared from artisan baguettes brushed with olive oil and toasted until crisp.

Beer Cheese Sauce for Pretzels (V)

Morgan Street Brewery

5 lb mild cheddar cheese
2 C all purpose flour
3 Tbsp tabasco
4 C heavy cream
4 C honey wheat beer
Salt and pepper

Heat up heavy cream to simmer, shred the cheese and mix with flour then add to hot heavy cream whisk to combine then add beer and tabasco. Add salt and pepper to taste.

Tomato Salad with Mozzarella, Thick-cut Bacon and Tomatoes Marinated in Balsamic Vinaigrette.

JON WHITAKER, MANAGER
International Tap House, Certified Cicerone

¾ C balsamic vinegar
2 C olive oil
1 clove fresh garlic, finely chopped
1 Tbsp brown sugar (honey may be substituted)
1 Tbsp Dijon® mustard
Salt
Pepper
3 vine-ripened tomatoes, sliced thick
½ red onion, chopped
6 oz thick cut bacon, cooked crispy and chopped
8 oz mozzarella cheese, sliced thick
Fresh basil, chopped

Add olive oil, vinegar, garlic, sugar, and mustard into bowl. Whisk until everything is incorporated and the mixture just barely clings to a spoon. Add salt and pepper to taste. At this time you can adjust the oil, vinegar, sugar, salt or mustard, based on your preference for sweet versus salty versus savory, etc. Place your sliced tomatoes into a large resealable bag and add in the entire salad dressing mixture. Make sure all tomatoes are coated in the bag and refrigerate for 2-3 hours. Every half hour, adjust the mixture to make sure all tomatoes get an even amount of the marinade. Remove tomatoes from bag and arrange them as desired on a serving plate/tray. Be sure to leave the unabsorbed marinade in the bag. We are just looking to enhance the sweetness of the tomatoes and not overpower them with the dressing. Dress each tomato with a slice of mozzarella, then sprinkle the red onion, bacon and fresh basil as desired. Please note that all these can be adjusted based on your taste preference.

This is absolutely my favorite appetizer to make for a large dinner party and is often requested, regardless of the main course. I pair this meal with a bottle of the Belgian beer, Duchesse De Bourgogne. The beer is a Flanders Red-style ale and has distinct notes of balsamic vinegar. It is evenly balanced between sweetness and tart/sourness. The balsamic vinegar in the recipe will really enhance the natural sweetness of the tomato and enhance your enjoyment (well, I really enjoy this part) of a great sweet/salty combo when the bacon and mozzarella are added. It eats somewhat light and your palate will actually stay somewhat clean when you are finished.

Restaurant Main Dishes

Sole Meuniere

CHEF BRYAN CARR
Avenue Restaurant

2 (6 oz) filets of sole
3 oz whole butter
Flour for coating
1 scant handful chopped parsley
1 oz. fresh lemon juice
Salt and pepper

Heat a skillet large enough to accommodate fish. Meanwhile, lightly flour the fish. When skillet is hot, add a little vegetable oil or clarified butter, and half of the whole butter. Cook the fish over medium heat until nicely browned. Turn over and cook for 30 seconds on other side. Remove fish from skillet and hold on plates in a warm place. Pour cooking oil out of skillet and return skillet to the heat. Put remaining whole butter in the pan and cook until it begins to brown. Add lemon, parsley, salt and pepper and spoon over fish. Serves 2.

Rigatoni Sauce

ONESTO PIZZA & TRATTORIA

1 large onion, medium diced
1 red pepper and 1 green pepper, medium diced
1 Tbsp chopped garlic
½ tsp red pepper flakes
1 lb Italian Pork sausage
40 oz tomato filets
1½ tsp dry basil
1 tsp dry oregano

Sweat together onions, peppers, garlic and red pepper flakes. Add sausage in chunks. Cook until brown. Add dry seasoning. Add tomatoes. Simmer until reduced by one-fourth (1-2 hours.) Serve with the pasta of your choice.

Cyrano's Veggie Burger Recipe (V)

Cyrano's Restaurant

1 (16 oz) can Bush's Vegetarian Baked Beans®
½ C cooked quinoa
½ C cooked brown rice
½ C uncooked old-fashioned oats
1 C cornbread stuffing mix (Pepperidge Farms® preferred brand), plus more as needed
1 (16 oz) pkg frozen mixed vegetables (cauliflower, broccoli, carrots)
1 Tbsp fresh parsley
1 Tbsp soy sauce
½ C finely chopped onion
Salt and pepper

Chop vegetables in a food processor until fine, but still distinct, avoiding a one-color mush. In a large bowl, use hands to combine vegetables, beans, stuffing, onion, parsley, soy, salt and pepper, mashing beans. The mixture should be moist, but if it is too moist to hold together, add more cornbread stuffing (up to 2 cups.) Cover and refrigerate for at least 1 hour. Scoop out 1 cup and shape into large burgers; repeat with remaining mixture. Heat a film of oil in a nonstick or well-seasoned skillet. Add burgers, cook each side until crispy and burger is heated through. To serve "Cyrano's style," toast buns and top with cooked burgers, lettuce, tomato, red onion and drizzle with remoulade. Serve with a pickle on the side. Serves 4.

Pasta Ligurian

CHEF D. SCOTT PHILLIPS
Balaban's

1 lb pasta, linguine or fettuccine
4 oz of extra virgin olive oil
4 cloves or 2 heaping Tbsp of minced fresh garlic
5 oz of small cubed feta cheese
3½ oz diced sun-dried tomatoes, oil drained
5 oz coarsely chopped walnuts
¼ tsp red pepper flakes
1 oz finely chopped fresh parsley
1 lb shrimp, peeled and deveined

Bring large saucepan of salted water to boil and add pasta cook till al dente, approx. 5-7 minutes. Drain. In a large skillet, heat oil with red pepper flakes on medium heat to flavor oil. Add shrimp and sauté till done, 1-2 minutes. To skillet, add all remaining ingredients, reserve parsley, and heat till hot. Add pasta and toss; season to taste. Garnish with chopped parsley. Serves 4.

Jumbo Lump Crab Cake Burger with Creamy Coleslaw

ZODIAC CAFÉ AT NEIMAN MARCUS
from Neiman Marcus Cooks by Kevin Garvin

Ingredients for Coleslaw:

2 C mayonnaise

¼ C apple cider vinegar

2 Tbsp sugar

2 Tbsp chopped fresh dill

2 tsp Dijon mustard

1 tsp caraway seeds

½ Tbsp prepared horseradish (optional)

½ tsp celery seeds

½ tsp celery salt

½ tsp kosher salt

½ tsp onion salt

½ tsp freshly cracked black pepper

6 C shredded white cabbage

½ C grated carrot

Ingredients for the crab cake burgers:

1 lb jumbo lump blue crabmeat

1 large egg, beaten

¼ C mayonnaise

1 scallion, thinly sliced (white and green parts, about ¼ cup)

2 Tbsp minced fresh Italian parsley

1 tsp Dijon mustard

1 tsp Worcestershire® sauce

Dash of Tabasco® sauce or to taste

1 Tbsp Old Bay Seasoning®

5 Tbsp fine plain bread crumbs

Vegetable oil, for sautéing

1 Tbsp softened butter

4 soft brioche rolls

Lettuce leaves and tomato sliced, for garnish (optional)

To prepare the creamy coleslaw, place the mayonnaise and vinegar in a mixing bowl and add the sugar, dill, mustard, caraway seeds, horseradish, celery seeds, celery salt, kosher salt, onion salt and pepper. Mix together the shredded cabbage and carrot in a large bowl, pour the coleslaw dressing over, and mix well. Adjust the seasonings and keep refrigerated until ready to serve.

To prepare the crab cake burgers, place the crab meat on a cookie sheet and spread it out evenly. Pick through carefully to remove any shell or cartilage. Return the crabmeat to a bowl. In a separate bowl, combine the egg, mayonnaise, scallion, parsley, mustard, Worcestershire sauce, Tabasco and Old Bay seasoning and mix gently with a fork. Fold the mixture into the crabmeat. Sprinkle the bread crumbs on the mixture and gently stir to combine with a fork so as not to break up the lumps of crab. Form the crab cake mixture by hand into 4 patties, around 1" high and 4" wide. Place on a plate, cover with plastic wrap and reserve in the refrigerator until ready to cook. Preheat the oven to 200 degrees. Pour ¼ inch of vegetable oil into a large skillet set over medium heat. When the oil is hot, gently add the crab cakes and sauté for about 2 minutes on each side. Transfer the crab cakes to a plate lined with paper towels. Keep warm in the oven while assembling the sandwiches. Lightly butter the soft rolls and warm in oven. Place crab cake on each warm buttered roll and serve ½ cup of the coleslaw on top of the crab cakes (with lettuce and tomato, if you like.)

Southwest Breakfast Strata (V)

CHEF JON HOFFMAN
White Box Eatery

8 slices of white bread, cubed
1 lb shredded cheddar cheese
1 C roasted red onion
5 Fresno peppers, seeded and thinly sliced
7 C 2% milk (or milk of your choice)
12 eggs, beaten
2 tsp dry mustard powder
2 Tbsp kosher salt
1 tsp black pepper

In a large mixing bowl, combine the bread, cheese, onion and peppers. In a separate bowl, beat the eggs with the milk. Add in the mustard powder, salt and pepper and whisk together until fully incorporated. Pour the wet ingredients over the dry ingredients and mash together by hand. Place the mixture into a greased 9" x 13" pan. Cover with plastic wrap, then with aluminum foil and bake at 350 degrees for 35 minutes. Remove the plastic wrap and foil and bake uncovered an additional 10 minutes until the top is browned. Cut and serve hot with black bean and corn salsa (recipe below.)

Black Bean and Corn Salsa (V)

CHEF JON HOFFMAN
White Box Eatery

2 C yellow corn kernels
1 C black beans, cooked
1 C cherry tomatoes, quartered
2 C lightly packed baby arugula
¼ C chopped cilantro
¼ C olive oil
Salt and pepper to taste

Combine all ingredients in a mixing bowl and toss together gently. Serve as a garnish to the strata immediately.

Chicken Spiedini Prosciutto

CORY CHIODINI
Zia's On the Hill Restaurant

2 lbs of chicken tenders
1 C Zia's Sweet Italian Salad Dressing®
1 C Italian seasoned breadcrumbs
3 C Zia's White Wine Lemon Butter Sauce®
1 C fresh sliced mushrooms
1 C diced Prosciutto ham
1 C shredded Provel cheese

Combine chicken and salad dressing in a zip top bag and marinate for 1½ hours. Discard marinade. Toss chicken in breadcrumbs and skewer 8 oz. on each skewer. Grill over medium heat until juices run clear, approximately 12 minutes. Bring Zia's wine sauce to a simmer over low heat. Add mushrooms and Prosciutto. Cook until mushrooms are tender. Remove chicken from skewers to a serving plate. Top with cheese and sauce; garnish with additional cheese (may prepare in the oven at 350 degrees. Do not use skewers, but instead arrange in oven safe dish and bake for approximately 20 minutes.)

Try adding additional seasonings to enhance your entrée
Capers and dill to fish
Dijon mustard for beef and chicken
Sage for chicken and veal
Garlic and black pepper for beef or chicken soto
Also try adding fresh vegetables for that unique dish

Chicken Pot Pie

Luvy Duvy's Restaurant

1 lb butter
6 Tbsp all purpose flour
2 C chicken broth
Pinch of salt and pepper
½ tsp thyme
1½ C heavy cream
1 lb cooked white chicken, shredded
Equal parts vegetables (peas, carrots, green beans, potatoes, etc.), frozen or fresh

Preheat oven to 425 degrees. To start, make a roux: in a heavy pot, melt butter. Stir in flour. Once stirred in, add 2 cups of chicken broth, pinch of salt and pepper, and stir all this nicely together, but don't let brown. Add the remaining ingredients and place in your dish of choice. Bake for 15 minutes until the center is warm. Take out and add biscuits (either canned or homemade.) Place back in oven at 425 degrees until biscuits are golden brown. Enjoy and warm up.

Brew House Turkey and Salsiccia Meatloaf

Ferguson Brewing Company

1 lb ground turkey
1 lb ground Salsiccia sausage
1 C Italian bread crumbs
5 oz. frozen spinach (1/2 box), chopped
1 egg
1 C red bell peppers, diced
1 C yellow onions, diced
1 Tbsp granulated garlic
1 tsp black pepper
1 tsp salt
Topping
1 C ketchup
¼ C brown sugar
1 Tbsp Worcestershire sauce

Preheat oven to 375 degrees. Combine all meatloaf ingredients in a large mixing bowl until thoroughly mixed. Transfer meatloaf mixture into a greased bread pan. Bake for 1 hour or until internal temperature reaches 170 degrees. Remove from oven. For topping: combine all ingredients in a small saucepan. Heat on medium-low temperature until sugar dissolves. Top meatloaf with topping and return to oven for 5 additional minutes. Remove from oven and let sit for 5 minutes. Turn out meatloaf to cutting board or baking sheet and slice ¾" slices. Serve immediately.

Curried Chicken Salad

Overlook Farm

2 C cooked cubed chicken
¼ C crumbled bacon
½ C halved grapes
½ C chopped pecans
1½ Tbsp curry powder
¾ C mayonnaise

Combine all ingredients; add salt and pepper to taste

Mole Sauce

Casa Del Mar

¼ C salad oil
2 C yellow onion, peeled, cored and medium chop
1 to 1½ C Poblano peppers, washed, seeded, cored, medium chop
½ C fresh garlic, peeled, whole
½ tsp ground cloves
3 Tbsp cumin, toasted and ground
1 Tbsp ground black pepper
1 C chicken base
3 C ground New Mex Chile Paste®
1 gallon water
½ C sugar
3 C Hershey's® Chocolate Chips

Roux
1 stick unsalted butter, melted and ¾ C flour, as needed, prepared, held at room temperature

Add oil to a suitable pot. Add onions, peppers and garlic to hot oil and sauté until starting to brown. Add water, cloves, cumin, black pepper, chicken base, sugar and New Mex paste, and bring to simmer. Puree until smooth with hand blender. Bring up to a low simmer. After simmering, whip in roux in small batches and return to simmer each time to check thickness. When thickened, simmer for 3-5 minutes, then remove from heat. Add chocolate in stages to melt without boiling. Remove from heat and chill properly. Will keep up to 4 days. Do not boil while reheating.

Risotto with Duck Confit

CHEF ADAM KARL GNAU
Acero Ristorante

1½C Carnaroli rice
1 small yellow onion (fine diced)
6 C (brodo) stock (a vegetable stock with the addition of Parmigiano Regiano rinds)
¾ C white wine
Butter as needed
1½ C Parmigiano Regiano
4 Tbsp Taleggio cheese
Salt to taste

In a heavy bottomed sauce or shallow stock, pot melt 3 Tbsp of butter and add onions. Cook on a low flame until the onion is translucent and soft. Add rice and allow to toast, stirring constantly. You will smell the aroma when ready. Add wine and allow to evaporate all the while slowly stirring. When the rice starts to dry, add a small ladle of the stock and stir in. As the stock evaporates, stir in more liquid (add desired pumpkin sauce toward the end of cooking.) Repeat this step until the rice is to the doneness you prefer and the consistency you desire. Take off flame and add in the Parmigiano, Taleggio and 3 more Tbsps butter. Serves 4.

Pumpkin Sauce

1 lb peeled pumpkin
½ yellow onion (large dice)
Water to cover by 2 inches
3 Tbsp butter
1 bay leaf
3 cloves garlic
Salt and pepper to taste

Melt the onion in butter till soft and translucent. Add the garlic till cooked. Add pumpkin, bay leaf and water. Bring to a boil, then down to a simmer and cook until pumpkin is tender. Place this mixture into a blender and blend till smooth. Chill immediately if not to be used right away.

Duck Confit

3 duck leg quarters
Salt and pepper
Duck fat to cover

Season duck with salt and pepper. Add duck to a medium-hot pan, skin-side down and brown till golden. Transfer the duck into a small pot and cover with the duck fat. Place on heat and allow small bubbles to form; place in a 200 degree oven. Cook until you can pull the thigh bone out. Check frequently, but should take at least 1½ hours. Flake the duck and top the risotto with it.

Tortilla Espanola (Spanish Omelet) (V)

BARcelona Tapas

3 Idaho potatoes, sliced ¼" thick
8 eggs
Vegetable oil
2 handfuls of fresh spinach
1 medium yellow onion, chopped
1 clove garlic, sliced
2 Tbsp olive oil
Salt and pepper to taste

In a large skillet over medium heat, add vegetable oil. Once oil is hot, add potato slices, onion and garlic. Cook until potatoes are soft. Drain the oil and combine potato mixture with beaten eggs. Add spinach (2 handfuls) and salt and pepper. In a large skillet, heat olive oil and combine potato/egg mixture and cook 4-5 minutes, flip and cook other side until both sides are lightly brown. (Internal temp 145 degrees.) Slice and serve.

Shrimp Chorizo with Sunchoke Yogurt, Granola, and Sunchoke & Raisin Relish

JOSH GALLIANO
Executive Chef

Granola Ingredients:

1¼ C rolled oats

1 C almonds, chopped

2 C sunflower seeds

⅓ C Benne Seeds

¼ C light brown sugar

1 tsp cinnamon, ground

½ tsp ginger, ground

½ tsp salt

¼ C cane syrup or sorghum

1 Tbsp canola oil

¼ C grated coconut

Mix together dry ingredients. Mix together wet ingredients. Combine, bake in a 250 degree oven for 45 minutes.

Sunchoke Relish

1 quart sunchokes, cut into chunks

1 onion, julienned

1 garlic, minced

2 Tbsp Melfor Honey Vinegar®

1 Tbsp honey

4 tsp ground turmeric

1 C white wine

1 C hot water

1 C golden raisins

Blanche the sunchokes in a pot of salted water. Once cooked to a toothsome point, remove from the water and shock in ice water. Steep the raisins in the white wine, hot water and turmeric. Sweat the onions and garlic in olive oil. Once translucent, add the raisins and its steeping liquid. Cook over medium-high heat to reduce by half. Once reduced, add the honey, melfor honey vinegar and sunchokes. Reduce until syrupy.

Shrimp Chorizo

2 lbs blue prawns, rough chopped

2 cloves garlic, minced

¼ tsp salt

¼ tsp smoked paprika

¼ tsp paprika

Pinch cayenne

In a food processor, combine all ingredients. Puree half of the mixture. Combine with the rest of the shrimp mixture. Place the shrimp chorizo mixture in silicone spherical molds (available at your local cooking store), vacuum seal the molds and rest in the refrigerator overnight. Heat a circulating water bath to 127 degrees. Cook the shrimp molds for 40 minutes, then shock in ice water.

Sunchoke Yogurt

1 lb sunchokes, peeled
2 C organic yogurt
1 tsp tahini
½ tsp lemon juice
Salt and pepper, to taste

Cook the sunchokes in a large pot of salted water until tender. Once tender, drain the sunchokes. Place the sunchokes in a blender along with the tahini, lemon juice and yogurt. Puree on high until smooth. Season with salt and pepper.

Assembly Directions

Makes 10
Sicilian olive oil
Micro fennel

Place the yogurt on the base of a plate in a circular motion, building up the sides to resemble hummus. Place the relish along the side of the yogurt in the inside circle. Place 3 one-inch cylinders of shrimp chorizo around the relish, then sprinkle with the sunflower seed granola. Drizzle with Sicilian olive oil and micro fennel.

Wicked Good Shrimp

CHEF WIL PELLY

3 oz Worcestershire sauce
3 oz water
3 oz lemon juice
1 Tbsp minced shallot
1 tsp minced garlic
1 Tbsp chives cut at 45 degree angle (optional)
14 21 to 25 count sized shrimp, cleaned
1 tsp cracked black pepper
1½ tsp cajun seasoning
¼ lb unsalted butter (brew)

Combine all ingredients except shrimp and butter in a skillet large enough to accommodate. Bring to a simmer. Add shrimp in one layer. After about 1 minute, turn all shrimp and let cook for 30 seconds. Remove shrimp and continue to simmer sauce till reduced to almost half. Remove pan from heat and add butter. Swirl the pan around until all butter has melted. Cover shrimp with sauce top with chives and serve with bread.

Big Sky Café Salmon Burger

CHEF DOMINIC WEISS
Big Sky Café

2 lbs raw Loch Duart salmon
2 Tbsp horseradish
1 Tbsp kosher salt
1 pinch black pepper
2 Tbsp fresh lemon juice
1 egg
3 Tbsp extra strong dijon mustard
½ C fine diced shallots

Preheat oven to 350 degrees. Cut salmon into small chunks. Pulse salmon with all ingredients aside from shallots in a food processor until combined and resembles texture of ground beef. Mix in diced shallots with a rubber spatula until well distributed. Divide mixture into six equal portions onto a well-greased baking sheet. Shape each portion into patty (mixture will be loose and a bit sticky.) Bake at 350 degrees convection for approximately 10 minutes just until patties firm and cook through.

Smoked Tomato Mayonnaise
1 C mayonnaise
1 med tomato (smoked and diced)
4 Tbsp fine diced gherkin pickles
2 Tbsp diced red onion
2 tsp fresh lemon juice
2 tsp honey
Salt to taste

Mix all ingredients together until well combined. Place hot salmon burger on your favorite bun (grilled) with arugula, top with Smoked Tomato Mayonnaise.

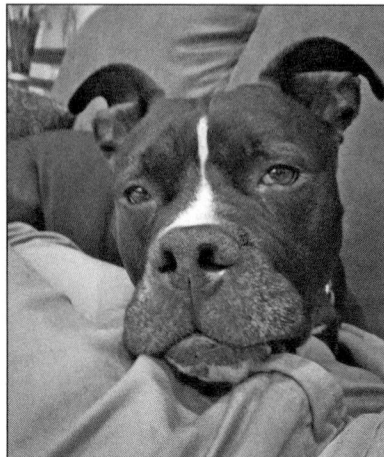

Stray Rescue – Bob Seger

Smoked Egg Salad (V)

MIKE EMERSON
Pappy's Smokehouse

12 eggs
Apple wood or cherry wood chips
¼ to ½ C marjoram mayonnaise (see below)
¼ C minced shallots
1 stalk celery, diced
4 Tbsp capers
1 Tbsp fresh parsley, chopped
Salt and freshly ground black pepper

Marjoram Mayonnaise Ingredients
1 large egg
1 Tbsp tarragon vinegar
½ C olive oil
½ C vegetable oil
1 Tbsp fresh marjoram, chopped
½ tsp salt
Pinch freshly ground white pepper

In a food processor, blend the egg and vinegar for 10 seconds. With the processor running, slowly pour the oils through the feed tube and process until emulsified (should the mixture become too thick, with the machine running, add water, 2 teaspoons at a time.) Add the marjoram, salt and pepper and pulse to blend. Transfer to an airtight container and refrigerate for at least 30 minutes before using.

Egg Salad Directions
Place the eggs in a medium saucepan and cover with water by 1 inch. Bring to a boil, reduce the heat to medium-low and cook the eggs at a bare boil for exactly 10 minutes. Drain and rinse the eggs under cold running water, then place them in an ice bath to cool. When chilled, peel the eggs and cut them in half lengthwise. Take a handful of wood chips and scatter them in the bottom of a stove-top smoker (or into a hot grill.) Heat the chips over medium-low heat until smoky, about 10 minutes. Place 16 egg halves rounded side down on the rack of your smoker; reserve 8 halves. Smoke for about 45 minutes. Allow to cool. Dice all of the eggs (smoked and not-smoked) and then chill them. In a medium bowl, combine the diced eggs with ¼ cup marjoram mayonnaise. Add the shallots, celery, capers and parsley, and stir carefully to combine. Additional mayonnaise may be added, 1 tablespoon at a time, to reach the desired consistency. Adjust the seasoning to taste. Cover and refrigerate until ready to serve.

Sweet & Salty Roasted Chickpeas (V)

REBECCA WEINGART
Head Chef, Pura Vegan

1 (15-ounce) can chickpeas, rinsed and drained
1 Tbsp olive oil
1 Tbsp balsamic vinegar
1 Tbsp soy sauce
1 tsp maple syrup

Preheat oven to 400. Combine chickpeas, olive oil, balsamic vinegar, soy sauce, and syrup on a baking sheet lined with parchment paper. Bake for 30 minutes, being careful not to burn. Stir the chickpeas halfway through baking.

Note: For a gluten-free option, use Bragg's liquid aminos or gluten-free tamari in place of the soy sauce.

Linguine with Sea Scallops

Trattoria Toscana

1 lb sea scallops
1 lb linguine
3 cloves of garlic, sliced thin
1 oz sundried tomatoes
1 oz vodka
8 Tbsp olive oil
1 oz butter
½ C heavy cream
1 C chicken stock
2 shallots, chopped
4 Tbsp black truffles
1 C flour
1 C Parmigiano Reggiano
1 pinch red pepper flakes
Salt to taste
8 leaves of fresh parsley, chopped

Lightly flour scallops. Heat half of the oil in a skillet. Sauté both sides of the scallops until lightly browned. Set aside. For sauce, heat the other half of the oil in a skillet. Sauté the shallots, garlic, sundried tomatoes and truffles for about 5 minutes. Add vodka and cook another 2 minutes. Add the butter, cream, chicken stock, half the parsley, half the cheese, salt, and red pepper flakes. Reduce on slow heat for about 8-10 minutes. Set aside. In lightly salted boiling water, cook pasta for about 8 minutes, until al dente (firm). Strain. Toss in scallops and sauce. Place on plate with scallops on top. Add remaining parsley and cheese to serve.

Shrimp and Grits

GAMLIN WHISKEY HOUSE

2 C heavy whipping cream
2 C chicken stock
1½ tsp kosher salt
1 C coarse ground cornmeal
½ tsp freshly ground black pepper
4 Tbsp unsalted butter
8 oz mild white cheddar, shredded
8 oz pepper-jack cheese, shredded

Place the cream, stock and salt into a large, heavy-bottomed pot over medium-high heat and bring to a boil. Once the mixture comes to a boil, gradually add the cornmeal while continually whisking. Once all of the cornmeal has been incorporated, decrease the heat to low and cover. Remove lid and whisk frequently, every 3 to 4 minutes, to prevent grits from sticking or forming lumps. Make sure to get into corners of pot when whisking. Cook for 20 to 25 minutes or until mixture is creamy. Remove from heat, add the pepper and butter, and whisk to combine. Once the butter is melted, gradually whisk in the cheeses, a little at a time.

Tomato Stock
1 C Zing Zang
1 C chicken stock
1½ tsp horseradish, grated
1 tsp lemon juice
½ tsp celery seed
1 Tbsp Worcestershire® sauce

Combine ingredients.

Shrimp and Grits
8 shrimp
4 oz applewood smoked bacon, sliced
2 oz onion, chopped
2 oz red bell pepper, chopped
2 oz green bell pepper, chopped
2 oz yellow bell pepper, chopped
10 oz tomato stock
2 oz white cheddar
2 oz pepper-jack cheese
1 oz olive oil
2 C grits

Heat olive oil in a heavy-bottomed skillet over medium-high heat. Place bacon, onions and peppers in skillet and cook until half-way cooked. Add shrimp and cook for approximately 2 minutes. Add tomato stock. Reduce by one-fourth. Place grits in an oven safe bowl. Pour shrimp mixture over. Sprinkle cheese over the top and place in oven until cheese is melted. Serve.

Bowtie Jack Pasta

Hawthorne Inn

⅔ qt. half and half
3 tbsp margarine
1 tbsp freshly minced garlic
8 oz grilled chicken, cut into strips
1 lb shrimp, peeled and deveined
¼ C sun-dried tomatoes, julienne
¼ lb. crisp, crumbled bacon
4 oz crumbled gorgonzola cheese
1 lb cooked bowtie pasta
1 C fresh grated Parmesan
Salt and pepper
Fresh chopped scallions

In a large saucepan, combine Half and Half, margarine, garlic, shrimp, grilled chicken and sun-dried tomatoes. Cook over high heat until cream begins to rise. Add gorgonzola and cooked pasta. Continue cooking until cream begins to rise again. Slowly toss in Parmesan until desired consistency. Add salt and pepper to taste. Garnish with fresh chopped scallions.

Wild Flower's Signature Garlic Chicken

Wild Flower Restaurant in Central West End

2 (8 oz) boneless organic chicken breasts
4 oz of cream cheese
2 tsp roasted garlic, chopped
1 tsp of chives, chopped
Olive oil
1 C organic flour
2 free range eggs
2 C Panko® bread crumbs
Breading – use separate containers for each
Organic flour
Egg wash (3 eggs, 3 Tbsp milk, pinch of salt)
Panko bread crumbs

Pound out chicken breasts to 1/8". Blend cream cheese, roasted garlic and chives. Add cream cheese mix to center of the chicken breast and fold sides. Roll in flour, egg wash and then bread crumbs. Add olive oil to skillet and pan sear all sides until crisp on the outside. Place in a casserole dish and finish in oven at 350 degrees for approximately 30-40 minutes (final temp should be 165 degrees.)

Serve with your favorite vegetable and starch.

Pork Tacos

CHEF REX HALE
360

1 lb pulled smoked pork shoulder
12 (3½") flour tortillas
Korean barbecue sauce, to taste (recipe to follow)
2 C kimchi (recipe to follow)
1 C pickled cucumber (recipe to follow)

Korean Barbecue Sauce

4 oz Korean fermented hot pepper sauce
6 oz sugar
6 oz soy sauce
4 tsp rice wine vinegar
4 tsp sesame oil

Combine all ingredients in a stock pot and bring to a quick simmer. Remove from heat and chill.

Pickled cucumber

1 each English cucumber peeled, seeded and thinly sliced
2 Tbsp rice wine vinegar
2 Tbsp sugar
½ tsp Serrano chili, seeded and minced
2 tsp sea salt

Place all the ingredients in a container and chill for several hours.

Kimchi

1 head green cabbage, about 1 lb finely shredded
2 oz sea salt
4 oz rice wine vinegar
1 Tbsp sugar
2 Tbsp Sriracha hot chile paste
1" blade fresh ginger, peeled and grated
2 cloves garlic minced
2 scallions, sliced thin on a bias
2 carrots julienne
2 oz soy sauce
1 oz sesame oil

Toss cabbage in the salt and set in a colander off to the side and allow to wilt for about 2 hours. In the meantime, mix all other ingredients and hold in a large mixing bowl. Rinse salt from the cabbage with several changes of water and press dry. To finish, mix the dressing with the cabbage and place in a container; add enough water to cover if necessary. To assemble tacos, heat the pork in the barbecue sauce, stirring gently until hot throughout. Divide between the 12 warm tortillas, top with kimchi and pickled cucumbers, then garnish with daikon sprouts. Serves 4.

Seared Wild Alaskan King Salmon with Succotash and Sherry Vinegar Glaze

CHEF REX HALE
The Restaurant at the Cheshire

6 Tbsp unsalted butter
36 pearl onions, roasted and peeled
¾ C half-rendered, thick-cut smoked bacon
1½ C freshly shucked corn kernels
18 heirloom cherry tomatoes, halved
1½ C cleaned crowder peas or other fresh shelling beans or peas
2 Tbsp minced fresh garlic
2 oz hard apple cider
3 oz heavy cream
3 oz grated Parmesan
Sea salt and freshly ground black pepper, to taste
1 oz Micro basil
6 center-cut 4 oz King Salmon filets
Sherry vinegar glaze and extra virgin olive oil

Season the filets of King Salmon and sear over high heat in 2 Tbsps olive oil while cooking to medium. Sauté the vegetables, bacon and garlic in butter. Deglaze with hard apple cider and add cream. Reduce, add Parmesan cheese and season to taste with salt and pepper. Add micro basil. When the fish is cooked, rest the filets on top of the succotash. Drizzle the plate with sherry vinegar glaze and extra virgin olive oil and garnish with micro basil. Serves 6.

Red Curry Chicken Salad

LISA SLAY
Executive Chef Remy's Kitchen and Wine Bar

2½ lbs baked boneless skinless chicken breast
1 C mayonnaise
2 Tbsp Vindaloo paste (an Indian curry seasoning)
2 tsp minced garlic
1 tsp salt & pepper
2 oz white wine
2 oz roasted raw meats pistachios
2 oz golden raisins
4 oz minced yellow onion
4 oz chopped celery

Bake chicken ahead of time and let cool. In a large bowl, combine the mayonnaise, vindaloo paste, garlic, salt and pepper and wine and whisk together until thoroughly combined. With a rubber spatula, fold in the pistachios, raisins, onions and celery. Dice up the baked chicken and mix into the salad. Chill and serve.

Restaurant Side Dishes

Couscous Risotto (V)

CHEF CASSY VIRES

3 Tbsp olive oil
1 onion, diced
½ C shallots, chopped
4 C Israeli couscous
2 C white wine
2 C vegetable stock
1½ C butternut squash, shredded
1½ C Swiss chard, chopped
1 C heavy cream
1 C Parmesan cheese, freshly grated
3 Tbsp unsalted butter
2 Tbsp Italian parsley, chopped

Heat the olive oil in a large pot over medium heat. Once the oil is hot, add the onion and shallots and saute until soft, but not browned. Stir in the couscous and season with salt and pepper. Add wine, scraping any browned bits from the bottom of the pot, and stir until all wine has evaporated. Add stock and simmer until the liquid is reduced by half. Gently fold in the squash and Swiss chard, then add heavy cream. Cook over medium heat until creamy and thickened. Stir in Parmesan, butter and parsley, and continue stirring until well blended. Adjust seasoning and serve immediately. Garnish with additional Parmesan, if desired. Serves 8.

Honey Bacon Brussels Sprouts

Nathalies Restaraunt

4 C brussels sprouts, trim ends and cut in halves or quarters as desired
½ lb bacon, dice bacon and brown, reserving bacon fat
¼ medium red onion, sliced
Pinch of crushed red pepper (optional)
3 Tbsp honey

Heat 3 tablespoons bacon fat in large skillet on medium-high heat. Add onions and crushed red pepper, and saute for 1-2 minutes. Add sprouts, bacon and honey; stir to coat with fat and honey, and cook about 5 minutes, only stirring a few times so sprouts have time to brown between stirring. Sprouts are done when just tender and nicely browned. Season with salt and pepper to taste.

Mud House's Cranberry Apricot Chutney (V)

The Mud House Coffee and Kitchen

½ C yellow onion, small dice
4 garlic cloves, minced
1½ Tbsp ginger, peeled and minced
1½ Tbsp vegetable oil
1 C dried apricots, small dice
1 C dried cranberries, small dice
1½ C water
¾ C red wine vinegar
½ C granulated sugar
1 tsp kosher salt

Cut and measure out all ingredients as specified above. Set a medium, heavy-bottomed saucepan on medium heat. Add oil, onions, garlic and ginger. Stir until onions begin to become translucent. Add rest of the ingredients and lower heat to medium-low. Simmer, stirring occasionally,until almost all the liquid is absorbed, about 15 minutes, or until desired consistency is reached.

Yields about 2 cups. Recipe may be easily doubled. This sweet and tangy chutney pairs well with cheese, pork, chicken or turkey. We use it on our sandwich "The Goat."

Greek Salad (V)

Epic Pizza and Subs

Romaine
2 oz feta cheese
1 oz Pepperoncini's
2 oz chopped Kalamata Olives
Cucumbers
Tomatoes

Fill large salad bowl with fresh romaine. Top with feta cheese, chopped Kalamata olives, sliced cucumbers, sliced tomatoes, and pepperoncini slices. Best served with a light vinaigrette. Epic's favorite is a lemon vinaigrette dressing.

Pickled Green Tomato Relish (V)

RICK LEWIS
Executive Chef

7 lb green tomato, medium dice
5 yellow onions, medium dice
2 yellow bell peppers, medium dice
4 tsp salt
4 C apple cider vinegar
4 C sugar
1 tsp celery seed
2 tsp mustard seed

Place all of the ingredients except veggies into a pot and bring to a boil. Pour the boiling pickling liquid over the diced vegetables and refrigerate for two days.

Smoked Apple Butter (V)

BEN ANDERSON
Chef at Grapeseed St. Louis

10 lbs Golden Apples
2 oz Lemon Juice
Zest of 2 lemons
3½ C Sugar

Core & halve the apples. Put the cores in a pot with the juice and zest from the lemon. Cover the cores with 4 cups of water and bring to a boil. Decrease to a simmer and cook for 1 hour, then strain and discard the solids.

Smoke the apples for 2 hours between 225 degrees F and 250 degrees F checking periodically to ensure smoke stays with the fruit. After 2 hours the apples should be golden brown and tender.

In a large pot, stir together the smoked apples, the strained apple broth, and the sugar. Cover and bring to a boil. Decrease to a simmer and cook gently for ½ hour. In batches, puree the apples until smooth. Return to the pot and cook for 20 minutes. Place in container and let cool. When cooled its ready for use.

Maple Mascarpone Cheesecake (V)

RYAN BUETTNER, EXECUTIVE CHEF
Vin de Set

8 oz cream cheese
5 oz pure maple syrup
16 oz mascarpone cheese
2 eggs
1½ oz sugar
2 apples, sliced
6 oz jar caramel sauce

In a mixer with a paddle attachment, beat cream cheese, mascarpone cheese and sugar until light and fluffy. Add maple syrup and incorporate into batter. Add eggs, one at a time, until incorporated. Line the outside and bottom of 6 three-inch ring molds tightly with aluminum foil all the way up to the top. Fill the molds with cheesecake batter and put into a water bath that comes halfway up the side of the molds. Cover with foil and bake at 350 degrees for 45-60 minutes. Remove from oven and let cool at room temperature. Place in the refrigerator, preferably overnight. Sauté apple slices in caramel and top the cheesecake. Garnish with powdered sugar, whipped cream, and fresh berries. Serves 6.

Vegan Chocolate Chip Cookies (V)

KAYLEN WISSINGER
Whisk: a Sustainable Bakeshop

½ C coconut oil
1 C brown sugar
¼ C almond milk
1 Tbsp vanilla extract
2 C flour
1 tsp baking soda
1 tsp baking powder
½ tsp salt
1 C vegan chocolate chips
2-4 Tbsp almond milk

Cream coconut oil and brown sugar in stand mixer. Add one-fourth cup almond milk and vanilla. Add in all the dry ingredients and mix until combined, then add vegan chocolate chips. The mixture will be crumbly. Add 2-4 tablespoons almond milk until the dough comes together. Preheat oven to 325 degrees. Bake for 8-12 minutes, but watch carefully -- ovens have hot spots and they take less time. Once the cookies are golden and a bit browned around the edges, they're ready. Cool for 10 minutes. Makes 8-10 cookies based on size.

Gingerbread Cookies with Royal Icing (V)

Colleen's Cookies

6 C all purpose flour
1 tsp baking soda
½ tsp baking powder
1 C unsalted butter
1 C packed dark brown sugar
4 tsp ground ginger
4 tsp ground cinnamon
1½ tsp ground cloves
1½ tsp salt
1 C molasses
2 large eggs

Sift together flour, baking soda and baking powder, and set aside. Cream butter and brown sugar until light and fluffy. Add ginger, cloves, cinnamon, cloves, salt, molasses, eggs and flour mixture to butter mixture, and mix well until combined.

Divide dough into three flatten disks, wrap in plastic wrap and chill two hours. Roll dough onto a floured surface to approximately 1/8" thickness. Cut out cookies using your favorite cookie cutters. Place on a cookie sheet lined with parchment paper, cover with plastic wrap and chill 15 minutes. Bake cookies at 350 degrees for 8-10 minutes, depending upon your oven. Once the edges of the cookies start to brown, place them on a cooling rack. Once cooled, decorate with royal icing, sanding sugars, etc. Makes approximately 3 dozen 2" cookies.

Royal Icing
2 large egg whites or more to thin icing
4 C sifted powdered sugar or more to thicken the icing
¼ C water or as needed
Food coloring (only a drop at a time)

Beat the egg whites until stiff. Add sugar and water, and beat for 1 minute more. If icing is too thick, add water. If it is too thin, add more sugar. The icing may be stored in an airtight container.

Summer Berry Shortcake (V)

CHEF REX HALE
The Restaurant at the Cheshire

3 C cake flour
1 C sugar
1½ Tbsp baking powder
1 tsp salt
¾ C whipped butter
3 eggs
¼ C milk
2 Tbsp vanilla extract
Berry filling (recipe below)
Whip 2 cups whipping cream with ¼ cup sugar.

Mix all dry ingredients. Cut butter into the flour. Whip eggs lightly. Add the eggs and milk, blending until smooth. Refrigerate for at least 30 minutes. When chilled, place shortcake dough on well-floured surface. Roll or pat it with hands. Cut with a biscuit cutter into six 4-inch shortcakes. Place on greased baking sheet. Preheat oven to 350 degrees. Bake shortcakes for 12 minutes. Slice in half when just out of oven. Spoon the berry filling on the bottom half of the shortcakes. Top with whipped cream. Dust the top crust with powdered sugar and garnish with a mint sprig

Berry Filling

3½ pints mixed local berries, blueberries, raspberries and blackberries, cleaned
1 C sugar
2 Tbsp Grand Marnier®

In a bowl mix 2 1/2 pints of the assorted berries together. Puree the remaining pint of berries in a food processor with the sugar and Grand Marnier. Pour over the berries and fold together.

Chocolate Banana Shake (V)

ANDY KARANDZIEF
Crown Candy Kitchen

3-6 oz scoops of vanilla ice cream
4 oz chocolate syrup
3-5 oz milk depending on the thickness
½ banana, sliced

Put all ingredients in a blender and mix slowly until all the lumps are gone. Add 1 heaping Tbsp malt powder to the mix for a malt if desired.

"Naughty Vicar" Shortbread (V)

The London Tea Room

8 oz sugar
8 oz salted butter
3 oz cornstarch
16 oz all purpose flour
1 oz Naughty Vicar tea
1 tsp vanilla extract
2-3 Tbsp sugar for top

Preheat oven 335 degrees. Grind the tea with the sugar in a food processor until it is as fine as you can get it. Cream the butter and sugar together in a mixer until smooth. Add vanilla. Slowly add the cornstarch and flour, and mix until well blended. Place dough on a floured surface and roll dough into a rectangle (similar to biscotti) about 10" long and 3" wide and about 1/2" tall. Make cuts along the rectangle approximately 1" wide and place on a greased baking tray about 2" apart. Score the tops of the dough with a fork and sprinkle top with sugar. Bake for approximately 20 minutes.

Baetje Farms Goat Cheese Cake (V)

CHEF REX HALE
360

2 lb cream cheese
1 lb fresh Baetje Farms® goat cheese
½ C seasonal fruit puree
¾ C granulated sugar
2 whole large eggs
3 egg yolks
1 Tbsp vanilla
½ C sour cream

Whip the cheeses in a mixer with paddle attachment. Scrape the bowl and add the sugar, continuing to mix and thoroughly incorporating the sugar. Add vanilla, sour cream and the eggs one by one. Mix until smooth and scrape the bowl to complete thorough mixing. Do not over mix, as the eggs will cause the batter to rise. Chill batter for 1 hour. Spoon batter into molds and bake in a water bath at 250 degrees for approximately 30 minutes. Allow to cool and remove from the molds. Top with fruit puree.

Banana Raisin Bread Pudding (V)
Three Monkeys

3 long French loaves
5 whole eggs
3 egg yolks
1 Tbsp salt
1½ Tbsp vanilla extract
3 C heavy cream
3 C half and half
3 C sugar
1 Tbsp butter
2 ripe bananas, mashed
1 C raisins

Cut bread in large cubes, set aside. For the custard, whip eggs, yolks, salt, and vanilla together. Set aside. Melt butter in a large saucepan, add cream and Half and Half, and bring up to temp. Mix in sugar slowly, stirring often, and bring to a low boil. Remove immediately. Slowly whipping (a hand blender works wonders), add cream mixture to eggs. Mash bananas and add to custard; mix well. Add raisins (if desired) and let stand, stirring often, until just warm. Add custard to bread cubes, mixing well, until all bread is soaked and combined. Transfer to a well-greased deep 9" x 12" pan. Wrap in foil and refrigerate overnight. Preheat oven to 375 degrees. Let pan come to room temp. Bake 50 min. Open foil in center, leaving edges covered, return to oven and bake 20-30 minutes until knife inserted in center comes out clean. Allow to cool 20-30 minutes before cutting. Serve with caramel sauce.

Oat Jam Bars (V)
The Wolf

3 C brown sugar
3 sticks butter
3 eggs
2 tsp vanilla
3¼ C flour
4½ C oats
1½ tsp baking soda
¾ tsp salt
17.5 oz jam (homemade or store bought)

Preheat oven to 350 degrees. With electric mixer, cream together brown sugar and butter. Add eggs and vanilla; mix well. In separate bowl sift together flour, oats, baking soda and salt. Stir creamed mixture and oat mixture together. Reserve 3-4 cups oat mixture; press remaining into 1/2 sheet pan. Spread with jam. Top with reserved crumbs. Bake at 350° for 15-20 minutes until brown and set. Makes 24 large bars.

celebrities recipes

Celebrities Starters

Split Pea Soup (V)

SUSIE CASTILLO, MISS USA 2003 AND SHANDI FINNESSEY, MISS USA 2004
www.pageantology.com

3 C dried split peas
8 C vegetable stock (This turns out to be 2 containers of the Pacific Organic Vegetable Broth. Get an extra container just in case you need more.)
3 bay leaves
1 tsp of cumin
1 tsp of coriander
1 Tbsp of Himalayan or Celtic sea salt
1 medium onion, minced
4 medium garlic cloves, minced
3 stalks celery, minced
4 medium carrots, sliced
Optional toppings:
Avocado
Heirloom tomatoes, diced
Extra Virgin Olive Oil
Fresh ground black pepper
Fresh parsley, minced

Put all ingredients in a large pot (you can sauté the onions, celery and carrots first or add them in directly if you want a fat free soup.) Bring to a boil and reduce heat to low. Simmer, covered for about 30-40 minutes (until all the veggies and split peas are soft,) stirring occasionally to prevent split peas from sticking to the bottom of the pot. Season to taste with the additional toppings if you wish. We like to let the soup sit in the pot for about 30 minutes after it's cooked so the flavors are more abundant.

Cinnamon Banana Smoothie (V)

SHANDI FINNESSEY, MISS USA 2004
www.pageanatology.com

One banana
½ – 1 C almond milk (depending on the thickness you prefer)
Cinnamon (to taste)

Blend all ingredients together. For a thicker consistency, add less almond milk.

Butternut Squash Soup (V)

TOMMY DIMELLA AND MADELEINE PICKENS
Chef at Del Mar Country Club and Mustang Monument

2 oz butter
2 C chopped butternut squash
2 C roasted butternut squash
½ C onions, chopped
1 C apples, chopped and peeled
1 C carrots, chopped
6 C of vegetable stock
1 C of heavy cream (optional)
2 oz butter (optional)

If using a bar blender, add the following to the blender. If using a stick blender, add the following to a large bowl. Season with salt. Season with Chinese 5 spice and curry paste or powder (optional.) Note: mix one cup of vegetable broth with curry, then add to soup. Blend with stick blender or bar blender. Puree to the consistency you desire. Add more stock if you want soup to be thinner.

Apricot Glazed Salami

LEISA ZIGMAN

2 lb kosher salami
4 Tbsp apricot preserves
2 Tbsp Dijon mustard

Preheat the oven to 375 degrees.
Score the salami by slicing across and downward with angled cuts, but don't cut completely through. Prepare the glaze: Mix together apricot preserves and mustard. Make it sweeter or more mustardy depending on your taste. The end color of the glaze should be a light orange and the consistency should be more of a sauce than a jam (not too thick, but not runny either.) Place the salami on the foil and place in the baking dish. Slather the salami with all of the glaze and wrap the foil around the sides of the salami. Bake in the oven for 30 minutes. After 30 minutes, take the salami out and spoon over the glaze from the bottom of the foil. Re-wrap the sides of the salami with foil and bake for another 30 minutes. It's done when you see a brown and sticky texture on top. Cut into quarters and toothpick each piece. Serve immediately. Use extra sauce for dipping.

Roasted Tomato Soup with Grilled Cheese Croutons

JAMIE DEEN
Celebrity Chef

3 lbs plum tomatoes, cut in half
1 Vidalia onion, cut into quarters
6 cloves garlic, smashed, but not peeled
3 Tbsp olive oil
1 Tbsp honey
Kosher salt and black pepper
1 qt chicken stock
1 Tbsp fresh Dill, chopped, plus more for garnish
Grilled cheese croutons (recipe follows)

Preheat oven to 425 degrees. Place tomatoes, onions and garlic on a heavy baking sheet. Drizzle with olive oil, honey and plenty of salt and pepper. Toss to coat. Roast in oven for 35-40 minutes, until the edges are soft and beginning to caramelize on the edges. Slip the garlic cloves out of their skins. Using a slotted spoon, scoop the vegetables, in batches, into a blender. Puree until smooth. Place the sheet tray on a burner and add about ¾ cup of stock to the pan. Scrape up any browned bits with a wooden spoon and bring the liquid to a simmer. Transfer to a large saucepan along with the remaining 3 ¼ cups stock and puree. Season well with salt and pepper and simmer 25 minutes. During the last few minutes, add dill. Serve with grilled cheese croutons and another sprinkle of fresh dill.

Grilled Cheese Croutons
4 slices sourdough bread, sliced about ½" thick
1 C grated sharp yellow cheddar cheese
2 Tbsp butter, softened

Heat a large, non-stick skillet over medium heat. Evenly sprinkle two slices of bread with cheese and sandwich each with a second of bread. Butter the outside of each sandwich and cook until golden on each side of the sandwich, about 3 minutes a side. Remove from pan and let rest for 1 minute before cutting with a serrated knife into 2 inch square croutons.

Stray Rescue – Wendy

Copycat 54th Street Gringo Dip (V)

JILL DEVINE
Y98 Radio Personality

1 lb Velveeta Queso Blanco®, cubed
1 C pepper jack cheese, shredded
½ C shredded Parmesan
16 oz container pico de gallo
1 C milk
1 tsp cayenne
10 oz frozen chopped spinach, thawed and drained

In a saucepan, warm the cheeses, pico, milk and cayenne. Stir well until completely melted. Add the spinach, taking care to separate the leaves. Serve with chips, on nachos or with waffle fries.

Blueberry Banana Muffins (V)

JOAKIM AND LAURA LINDSTROM
St. Louis Blues Hockey

1 mashed ripe banana
¾ C low fat vanilla yogurt
⅓ C light brown sugar
1 egg
¼ C canola oil
¾ C quick cooking oats
1 C all purpose flour
¾ C whole wheat flour
2 tsp baking powder
2 tsp cinnamon
½ tsp baking soda
¼ tsp salt
¾ C frozen blueberries (or you can also add strawberries, raspberries, peaches, etc. You can play around with it.)

Combine banana, yogurt, brown sugar, egg and oil in a large bowl. Add oats and allow to sit for 5-10 minutes. Combine dry ingredients. Add blueberries and dry ingredients to wet and stir until just combined. Put in paper lined muffin tin and bake in a preheated 375 degree oven, until tops are firm to touch (about 15 minutes.)

Pulled Pork

RIDLEY PEARSON
Best Selling Author

Brine
4 – 5 lbs pork shoulder
1 – 2 qts apple juice
1 C apple cider vinegar
¼ C sugar
1 Tbsp salt
Roasting liquid
1 pint apple juice
1 C water
1 Tbsp salt

Combine ingredients in large roasting pan. Mix well. Brine pork for 12-24 hrs. Refrigerate. Preheat oven to 225 degrees. Remove meat from brine and dry pork. Cook on grill on all sides until luscious brown (you can use a rub if you have a favorite,) Remove pork to roasting pan that can be covered, if possible, such as Le Creuset. If an open pan, then make an aluminum foil "tent" to cover. Combine roasting liquid mixture in roasting pan, place browned pork into pan and cover, or seal. Cook at 225 degrees for 6-8 hours, checking for meat to fall apart with fork. Remove pork when falling apart. Pull pork apart on carving board, removing fat (and feed to your dogs.)

Two options: Serve as-is with your favorite barbecue sauces at the table or pull the pork, empty the pan of juice, return pork to pan and mix in a single barbecue sauce.

Chicken Spectacular

JEREMY MACLIN
Former Mizzou Wide Receiver and current Wide Receiver for the Philadelphia Eagles

3 C chicken, cooked
1 pkg Uncle Ben's Combo Wild and White Rice®, cooked
1 (10.5 oz) can cream of celery soup
1 medium jar of sliced pimentos
1 medium chopped onion
3 – 4 (14.5 oz) cans French-style green beans, drained
1 C real mayonnaise
1 can sliced water chestnuts, drained
Salt and pepper to taste

Mix all ingredients together and bake at 300 degrees for 25-30 minutes.

Shrimp Boat Casserole

CHRISTINA LINGO-TABUCHI
Entertainer, The Shoji Tabuchi Show

¾ stick butter (no substitute)
1 small onion, chopped
½ cup bell pepper, chopped
½ C celery, chopped
½ can Cream of Mushroom soup
1 Tbsp garlic, chopped
1½ pounds of cooked, deveined shrimp
4 oz cream cheese
1 tsp salt
2 C cooked rice
1 – 2 C sharp cheddar cheese, shredded
1 can french fried onions

Sauté veggies in a half a stick of butter, salt and garlic; add soup. While the veggies are sautéing, melt one-fourth stick butter with cream cheese in the microwave for 2 minutes. Mix sautéed veggie mix and cream cheese mixture together adding the shrimp and cooked rice. Place into a 9" x 13" casserole dish and top with cheese and French fried onions. Bake at 350 degrees for 25 minutes. Serves 2.

The O'Brien-Mason Fat Burger

MARSHA MASON
Award winning actress

1 lb ground chuck (a must, not sirloin)
1 onion, finely diced
Dash Worcestershire® sauce
Dash Ketchup®
Salt and pepper
Dash garlic powder
Small pinch turmeric

Additional ingredients:
2 slices of bacon
1 Tbsp butter
Toppings of your choice

Mix all ingredients together and let sit for an hour to room temp. Fry up 2 pieces of bacon and remove from fat. Add 1 Tbsp of butter. Fry the patties in the hot oils about 3 to 4 minutes each side for medium rare. Toast buns, add some horseradish, if you like, and mustard and pickles if you are of a mind, and place on the bun. Rest for a minute, turning it over to make sure all the juices are going to both sides of the bun and dig in. You can even add the bacon if you feel like it. And always serve with a small green salad. A recipe from my pal, Jack O'Brien, with some additions from yours truly. Enjoy. Serves 2.

Smashed White Bean and Avocado Club (V)

JULIE TRISTAN
Morning Show host for 103.3 KLOU

2 (15-oz) cans white beans, rinsed and drained
2 Tbsp extra virgin olive oil
½ tsp kosher salt
¼ tsp black pepper
12 slices multigrain bread
1 small red onion, thinly sliced
1 cucumber, preferably Hothouse, seedless, thinly sliced; peeled, if desired
4 – 5 oz container sprouts (such as alfalfa, radish, broccoli or a combination)
2 avocados, pitted and thinly sliced

In a medium bowl, combine the beans, oil, salt, and pepper. Roughly mash the mixture with the back of a fork. Place 8 of the bread slices on a work surface. Divide the mashed beans among them. Top with the onion, cucumber, sprouts and avocado. Stack the open-faced sandwiches on top of one another, avocado-side up, to make 4 double-decker sandwiches. Top with the remaining 4 slices of bread. Serves 4. 🦴

Creamy Chicken Alfredo with Angel Hair Pasta

MERLIN IMAN
Actor, Comedian, Show Host

1 (16 oz) pkg angel hair pasta
1¼ lbs boneless, skinless chicken breasts, cut into 1" cubes
¼ tsp pepper
3 Tbsp olive oil
1 large carrot, diced
2 Tbsp butter
1 medium onion, chopped
1 celery rib, diced
3 large garlic cloves, minced
2 C heavy whipping cream
5 bacon strips, cooked and crumbled
3 Tbsp lemon juice
1 tsp Italian seasoning
1 C Parmesan cheese, shredded

Cook pasta according to package directions. Meanwhile, in a large skillet, sauté the chicken, salt and pepper in 2 tablespoons oil until no longer pink. Remove and keep warm. In the same skillet, sauté carrot in butter and remaining oil for 1 minute. Add onion and celery; sauté 3-4 minutes longer or until tender. Add garlic; cook for 1 minute. Stir in the cream, bacon, lemon juice and Italian seasoning. Bring to a boil. Reduce heat; simmer, uncovered, for 2-3 minutes or until slightly thickened, stirring constantly. Return chicken to the pan. Drain pasta; toss with chicken mixture. Garnish with cheese. Serves 6. 🦴

Curry Chilean Sea Bass on the Grill

MONICA ADAMS
Fox 2 News in The Morning

6 – 8 oz filet of Chilean sea bass
1 small yellow squash
1 small green zucchini
1 ripe red tomato
2 Tbsp Italian seasoning
1 Tbsp curry
1 tsp turmeric
1 tsp coriander
Black pepper (adjust to your liking)
Himalayan sea salt (adjust to your liking)

Prepare whatever ounce sea bass you want in foil. No need to spray or add oil, as the oils from the natural fats in the sea bass will come out and the fish will naturally cook in that oil. Season with a blend of curry, turmeric and cumin. I use hot curry to kick it up a notch. Slice a blend of green and yellow squash, and tomatoes. Season with Italian seasoning, oregano, pepper and a pinch of Himalayan sea salt (optional.) Arrange the vegetables in the same foil as the sea bass so it takes in the oils of the fish and cook with that same tenderness. Fold the foil like a taco with the seal slightly pinched together to encapsulate the fish and vegetables. Grill at low to medium heat. Temperature is dependent upon how you like your fish and the heat of your grill. I cook for no longer than about 10-15 minutes. I open the seal of the foil in the final few minutes and let the oils come out of the fish into the vegetables. Test your fish temperature (should be 135 degrees.) You will know your fish is done when it becomes opaque in color. Do not under or overcook this fish. Remember this is a meaty fish and will require some TLC since it is not a cut that is thin like most white fish.

Options: add garlic, onions, small tips of asparagus for extra flavor and vegetable options. Serve over your favorite grain, such as quinoa or saffron rice.

Biscuits 'n Gravy

REBECCA ROBERTS
Reporter, FOX 2 News
(recipe originally from Aunt Karen Miranda)

2 (1 lb) packages of Jimmy Dean® sausage (1 mild, 1 hot)
1 C flour (more or less)
3 – 4 C whole milk (more of less)
1 pkg of frozen Pillsbury® biscuits

Chop up and brown sausage in a large heavy skillet until no longer pink. Reduce heat to medium low. Do not drain. Sprinkle ½ cup flour over juices and whisk until thickened. Add 2 cups of milk, continue stirring. Add more flour to thicken; stir. Add more milk and flour as necessary until desired consistency is achieved. Cover with lid until ready to serve. Serve over biscuits.

Fanny's Chesapeake Bay-style Crab Cakes

BERNIE MIKLASZ
St. Louis Post-Dispatch, Sports Columnist

1 egg
2½ Tbsp mayonnaise
1 tsp dry mustard
½ tsp black pepper
1 tsp Old Bay® seasoning
2 tsp Worcestershire® sauce
Dash of Tabasco® or other red-hot sauce
1 lb back fin crabmeat (Note: you may substitute lump crab meat for back fin)
¼ C cracker crumbs
Vegetable oil for deep frying

In a mixing bowl, combine the egg, mayonnaise, mustard, pepper, Old Bay, Worcestershire and Tabasco, and mix until frothy. Place the crabmeat in a bowl and pour the mixture on it. Sprinkle the cracker crumbs onto the top of the crab and the mixture. Toss gently, being careful to avoid shredding those luscious lumps of crabmeat. Form the crab cakes by hand or with a scoop into rounded mounds that are about 3" wide and 1" thick. Pack it loosely. You don't want to squish the crabmeat and turn this into a pancake or fritter. I prefer to broil the cakes (preheated the oven first) until brown on both sides, turning once to cook evenly.

The cakes are delicious if you fry them. If that's your preference, heat the oil in a deep skillet or fryer to about 375 degrees. Deep fry the cakes, a few at a time, until golden brown on all sides, about 4 minutes. Remove and place on paper towels to drain. This is a family recipe that comes from my late grandmother, who specialized in Chesapeake Bay and Southern-style cuisine while cooking for all of us in her tiny kitchen home near Annapolis, MD. I have made this many times through the years for family and friends. 🦴

Mendocino Enchiladas

GARY ABELOV
Author and Certified Dog Behavior Consultant in St. Louis, MO

½ garlic clove or to taste
1½ Tbsp oil
½ C onions, chopped
½ C mushrooms, sliced
½ C zucchini, thinly sliced
2 C cooked chicken, shredded
6 large fresh flour or corn tortillas, cooked on skillet or in microwave
1 C Monterey Jack cheese, shredded or cut into small cubes
Salsa (see recipe below)
1 C cheddar cheese, shredded

Sour cream
Guacamole (see recipe below)
4 jalapeño peppers, thinly sliced (optional)

Sauté garlic in hot oil in wok or skillet. Add onions, mushrooms and zucchini, and lightly sauté. Remove from heat; mix in chicken. Place mixture in center of open tortillas. Top each with slices of Monterey Jack cheese. Pour some salsa over top of each. Fold edges of tortillas over filling. Sprinkle cheddar cheese on top of each tortilla. Place enchiladas on lightly greased cookie sheet. Run under broiler just until cheese melts. Watch carefully; don't let tortillas harden or brown. When cheese has melted, remove enchiladas from oven. Transfer to serving plates. Place two to three tablespoons of sour cream and guacamole on either side of plate. Garnish with jalapeño slices, if desired. Serve with refried beans and/or brown rice. Serves 4-6.

Salsa
5 large red chili peppers
¼ C onion, chopped
2 Tbsp oil
3 (14 – 16 oz) cans whole tomatoes, undrained
2 garlic cloves, peeled
½ tsp cumin
¼ tsp dried oregano leaves
1 tsp salt

Cut or tear peppers into pieces. Place in saucepan with water to cover; bring to boil. Cook until peppers are tender, about 15 minutes, then drain. Sauté onion in hot oil until golden, about five minutes: drain. Blend chilies, onion, tomatoes garlic, cumin, oregano and salt in blender until smooth. Transfer to saucepan. Simmer over low heat for 30 minutes, stirring occasionally.
Yield: about 1 cup

Guacamole
2 large ripe avocados
¼ C onion, chopped
1 tomato, chopped
½ tsp salt
Jalapeño pepper slices, to taste (optional)

Mash avocados. Add onion, tomato, salt and jalapeño slices, if desired. Mix well.
Yield: About 1 cup.

Lemon Rotini with Sausage

KATY JAMBORETZ
VP of Marketing and Communications, St. Louis Economic Development Partnership

1 lb rotini
2 Tbsp olive oil
½ tsp red pepper flakes
2 cloves of garlic
1 large onion, thinly sliced
½ C white wine
1 lb sweet Italian sausage
1 bunch broccolini (spinach and arugula also work well)
½ C grated Parmesan cheese
Zest and juice of 1 lemon
Black pepper
Shaved or grated Parmesan cheese for garnish

Cook pasta. In a large sauté pan, heat oil. Add garlic, red pepper and onion. Sauté until onion just begins to brown. Add half of the wine and deglaze pan. Add sausage and brown, then add rest of wine. Roughly chop broccolini and add to pan. Combine pasta with sauce. Add Parmesan, lemon juice and zest to pan. Season with salt and pepper. Top with a bit more Parmesan.

Cornmeal Fried Catfish

SHOJI TABUCHI
Shoji Tabuchi Theatre, Branson, Missouri

1 lb catfish, cut into 3 inch fillets
1 C yellow cornmeal
1 – 2 tsp All Season Salt, to taste
Large Ziploc bag
Cooking oil of choice, enough to fill deep pan or deep-fryer

Put cornmeal and All Season Salt into large Ziploc bag and shake to mix. Add each catfish fillet and shake in bag to coat with mixture. Heat cooking oil to 325 to 350 degrees. Ease pieces of fish into hot oil. Deep fry 5-8 minutes; fish fillets will start to float and turn golden brown when cooked. When cooked golden brown and crispy, remove fish from oil using slotted spatula dipper and drain off excess grease. Serve and eat while hot.

Note: Catfish may be substituted for Crappie or Bass Fillets. Mr. Tabuchi loves to fish and this is his favorite recipe.

Baked Stuffed Trout

SHOJI TABUCHI
Shoji Tabuchi Theatre, Branson, Missouri

1 cleaned Rainbow Trout with head on
1 sheet heavy duty aluminum foil
Lots of butter
1 Tbsp diced onion
1 Tbsp diced green bell pepper
½ tsp minced parsley
1 Tbsp chopped mushrooms
Salt and pepper to taste

Preheat oven to 375 degrees. On heavy duty aluminum foil spread lots of butter where you will put your trout. Place trout on buttered foil with head on and belly open. Spoon butter inside belly and spread inside. Stuff trout belly with diced onion, diced green peppers, minced parsley, and chopped mushrooms. Sprinkle with salt and pepper to preference. Wrap foil around Trout and Bake at 375 degrees for 25 minutes.

Grandma Jankowski's Chicken

JOE BONWICH
Journalist

1 (2½ to 3½ lb) chicken, cut up, or specific pieces as desired
1 to 2 Tbsp butter
1 small onion, chopped
1 small carrot, chopped
2 Tbsp chopped celery and leaves
Salt
Freshly ground black pepper to taste
1 tsp granulated sugar
3-4 Tbsp paprika (sweet Hungarian is best)
1 C water or chicken stock

Brown chicken on all sides in a small amount of melted butter in a large skillet. Discard excess fat, leaving some pan juices. Add onion, carrot, celery, salt and pepper to taste, sugar and paprika. Simmer for 30 minutes. Water at this time should not be necessary since the chicken and vegetables will create their own juices. Turn all the chicken pieces. Simmer for 30 minutes longer, and then remove chicken to a platter. Add water or chicken stock to the mixture in the skillet and mix well. Heat until mixture thickens; it can be used as a sauce for the chicken or for mashed potatoes or noodles.

Celebrity Side Dishes

Ginger Tahini Dressing (V)

SUSIE CASTILLO, MISS USA 2003
www.pageantology.com

5-inch piece of fresh ginger, peeled and chopped (use a potato peeler to peel ginger)
Juice of 1½ fresh lemons
3 garlic cloves
¼ tsp sea salt
3 Tbsp extra virgin olive oil
½ C raw tahini
1 tsp white balsamic vinegar
Dash of freshly ground pepper
½ C water

Start with the chopped ginger and water in a high-speed blender. Blend the ginger really well, then add all the other ingredients and blend until creamy. Taste the mixture and add more of whatever ingredient you think it needs more of. Custom make it to suit your taste buds. Pour the sauce into a recycled pasta sauce glass jar and store in the refrigerator.

Note: Can use as a salad dressing, a dipping sauce for veggies or as a sauce for quinoa and roasted veggie dishes.

Brussel Sprouts with Roasted Grapes (V)

MONICA ADAMS
Fox 2 News in the Morning

2 C brussel sprouts, cut in half (about 6 oz)
1 C red grapes
1 Tbsp olive oil
Sea salt and ground black pepper (to taste; optional)
1 Tbsp sliced raw almonds (for garnish; optional)

Preheat oven to 375°. Combine brussel sprouts, grapes and oil in a large bowl. Season with salt and pepper if desired; mix well. Arrange brussel sprouts mixture with brussel sprouts cut side down, on metal baking sheet. Bake for 15 to 20 minutes, or until brussel sprouts are golden brown on the cut side. Stir; continue baking for 10 to 15 additional minutes, or until tender when pierced with a fork. Top with sliced almonds (if desired).

When I was growing up in south Arkansas, the big city was Little Rock, and whenever we went, we tried to have a meal at Franke's cafeteria. I always remembered the eggplant casserole, one of the cafeteria's most famous dishes, and finally managed to get the recipe. This is great to make in the summer when home-grown eggplant is plentiful.

Franke's Cafeteria Eggplant Casserole (V)

GAIL PENNINGTON
St. Louis Post-Dispatch TV Critic

Gail loves dogs, but not quite as much as she loves cats. She lives with Oliver (pictured) and his reluctant companion, Sophie.

1 medium eggplant, peeled and chopped
1 medium onion, chopped
3 Tbsp butter, divided
1 (14.5 oz) can diced tomatoes, drained
1½ C grated American or Cheddar cheese
4 eggs, beaten
1 C cornbread crumbs (or crushed crackers)

Preheat oven to 350 degrees. Cook eggplant in salted water until tender; drain. Sauté onion in 2 tablespoons butter until soft. Add 2 cups cooked eggplant and tomatoes, and mash together. Mix in eggs, cheese and ¾ cup crumbs and check to see if more salt is needed; pour into greased 2-quart casserole dish. Melt remaining 1 tablespoon butter and mix with remaining 1/4 cup crumbs to top the casserole. Bake for 20-25 minutes until bubbling and browned. 🦴

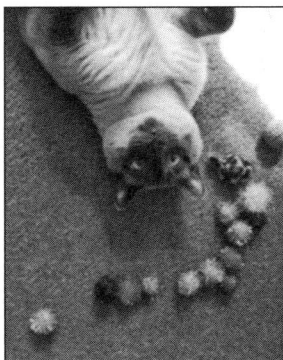

Oliver

Lemon Meringue Pie (V)

CHRISTINE BREWER
Grammy award winning soprano

1 pre-baked pie crust, fully baked and cooled completely

Lemon Filling
1 C sugar
¼ C cornstarch
¼ tsp salt
1½ C cold water
6 large egg yolks
1 Tbsp lemon zest, grated
½ C juice from 2-3 lemons
2 Tbsp unsalted butter

Meringue
1 Tbsp cornstarch
⅓ C water
¼ tsp cream of tartar
½ C sugar
4 large egg whites
½ tsp vanilla extract

Preheat oven to 325 degrees. For the filling: Mix sugar, cornstarch, salt and water in a large saucepan. Bring mixture to simmer over medium heat, whisking occasionally at beginning of the process and more frequently as mixture begins to thicken. When mixture starts to simmer and turn translucent, whisk in egg yolks, two at a time. Whisk in zest, then lemon juice and finally the butter. Bring mixture to a simmer, whisking constantly. Remove from heat. Place plastic wrap directly on surface of filling to keep hot and prevent skin from forming.

For the meringue: Mix cornstarch with water in small saucepan; bring to simmer, whisking occasionally at beginning and more frequently as mixture starts to thicken. When mixture starts to simmer and turn translucent, remove from heat. Let cool while beating egg whites. Mix cream of tartar and sugar together. Beat egg whites and vanilla until frothy. Beat in sugar mixture, 1 tablespoon at a time, until sugar is incorporated and mixture forms soft peaks. Add cornstarch mixture, 1 tablespoon at a time; continue to beat meringue to stiff peaks.

Remove plastic from lemon filling and return to very low heat during last minute or so of beating meringue to ensure filling is hot. Pour hot filling into baked pie shell. Using a rubber spatula, immediately distribute meringue evenly around edge and then center of pie to keep it from sinking into filling. Make sure meringue attaches to the pie crust to prevent shrinking. Use back of spoon to create peaks all over meringue. Bake pie until meringue is golden brown, about 20 minutes. Transfer to wire rack and cool to room temperature. Serve that day. Serves 8.

Yummy Peanut Butter Balls (V)

BARBARA ANGELINE DARKHORSE
Munchkin Ambassador to the Coroner of Munchkin Land in the Wizard of Oz

1 lb powdered sugar
1½ C peanut butter
½ C melted butter
3 C Rice Krispies® cereal
1 (12 oz) pkg chocolate chips
⅓ stick paraffin wax

Mix sugar, peanut butter, melted butter and Rice Krispies. Shape into balls. In double boiler, melt chocolate chips and paraffin wax. Dip balls in chocolate and lay on wax paper or in candy cups. Sprinkle with coconut, chopped nuts, your favorite spice or whatever you like. Makes about 60.

Quick and a Little Healthy Yogurt Pie (V)

SHERRY FARMER
Local Broadcast Personality/Emcee/Voice-Over Actress
Hostess of www.onstl.com "Stray Rescue Enrichment Dog of the Month" Stray Rescue Board Member

3 – 4 single-serving Yoplait Light Thick and Creamy®, flavors of your choice (I prefer using a mix of lemon, key lime and blueberry)
A little bit of Cool Whip®, to your liking
Gummy fruit slice or sprinkles
Pre-made graham cracker crust

Unwrap the pie crust, open the yogurt and combine in the crust. You can get crafty here by swirling the colors or keeping them all separate. Put a little dollop of Cool-Whip in the center and a cute fruit slice atop that. Easy! If you want to make it more kid-friendly, add more gummy slices, sprinkles or more Cool Whip.

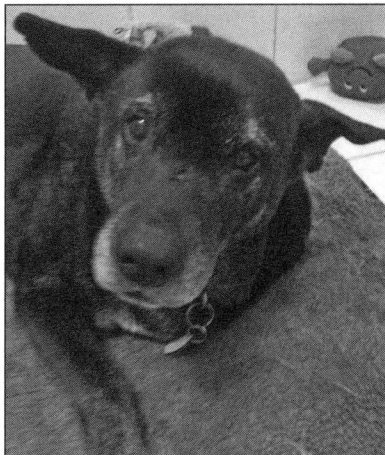

Stray Rescue – Oran

Almond Butter Cookies (V)

BIRGEN HARTMAN, DAUGHTER OF COMEDIAN PHIL HARTMAN AND ANIMAL ACTIVIST

1¼ C almond flour
¾ C almond butter
⅓ C honey
¼ C water
1 tsp baking soda
1 tsp vanilla
A dash of almond extract (optional)
1 tsp sea salt

Preheat oven to 350 degrees and line a cookie sheet with parchment paper. Combine dry ingredients first, then mix well with the rest of the ingredients. Spoon onto parchment paper-lined cookie sheet and bake for 8-10 min. When done, cool for 3-5 min before removing from the parchment paper. These are very soft, chewy cookies, so it helps to let them firm up a bit. Makes 1 dozen large cookies or 20 medium-sized cookies.

Approximately 7g net carb per cookie.

Frozen Lemonade Pie (V)

RANDY GRIM
Founder of Stray Rescue of St. Louis

1 premade graham cracker crust
½ gallon vanilla ice cream
6 oz. frozen lemonade concentrate
8-12 oz. frozen whipped topping, thawed

Let ice cream set out & soften for a few minutes. Mix lemonade & ice cream. Spoon into graham cracker crust. Frost with whipped topping. Cover with foil (if you can't figure out how to use plastic wrap) and freeze till firm.

LOCAL FARE

KISSES

Stl.

5¢

I ♥ RESCUES

Ravioli Tossed with Ozark Forest Shiitake Mushrooms and Walnuts in Budweiser Black Crown Brown Butter Cream Sauce

VITO RACANELLI JR.
Executive Chef of Taste of St. Louis

12 oz of cheese ravioli (fresh homemade or frozen package)
1 Tbsp light olive oil
1 C Ozark Forest shiitake mushrooms, sliced
2 Tbsp unsalted butter
½ tsp minced garlic
½ C chopped walnuts
1 bottle Budweiser Black Crown® beer
¼ C fresh squeezed orange juice
1 C heavy cream
½ C shredded Parmesan
½ tsp kosher salt
¼ tsp ground black pepper

Heat a large cast iron skillet over medium heat. Add olive oil and mushrooms. Lightly sauté mushrooms for 3-5 minutes, until they are soft.

Turn heat up to medium-high; add butter, garlic and walnuts. When the butter starts to smoke and there is a strong nutty aroma, (this should take about 1 minute), add Budweiser Black Crown and orange juice. Reduce heat to medium, and cook sauce for 4 minutes.

Add heavy cream, and cook for about 5 minutes, until sauce has thickened slightly. Add salt and pepper, and remove from heat. Boil ravioli in salted water for directed time on package. Strain ravioli from water. Add ravioli to sauce and toss together. Place on serving platter and top with shredded Parmesan.

Serves 4

Corn Fritters with Spicy Remoulade (V)

CHEF ROBERT TRAMPIER
St. Louis Country Club on Behalf of Taste St. Louis

2 Tbsp olive oil
1 C packed grated zucchini
¾ C fresh or frozen corn kernels
¼ C minced onion
2 tsp fresh thyme
2 tsp fresh cilantro
¾ C all purpose Flour
½ C + 2 Tbsp packaged corn muffin mix
2 Tbsp sugar
½ tsp salt
½ C milk
1 large egg

Set a mini fryer to 325 degrees. Sauté off vegetables, add herbs and season to taste. Cool. Mix dry and wet ingredients together, fold vegetable mixture into this. Scoop with a medium sized ice cream scooper, and gently place into the fryer oil set at 325 degrees. Cook for a few minutes, until fritters are done throughout.

Ingredients for Spicy Remoulade:
1 C mayonnaise
1 Tbsp cajun seasoning
Pinch of cayenne pepper
½ a lemon, juiced
Fresh chopped chives and parsley

Combine all ingredients and chill for 1 hour before serving.

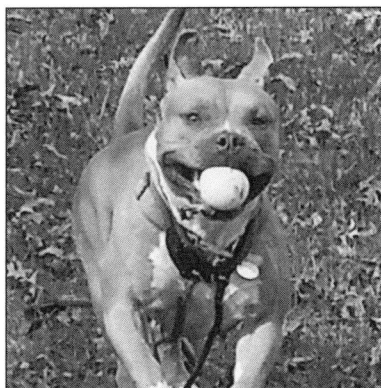

Stray Rescue – Narnia

Crazy Corn (V)

COMPLIMENTS OF CHEF DAVE ROOK
Bishop's Post

4 C mayonnaise
1 Tbsp granulated garlic
1 Tbsp black pepper
1 C milk
8 ears cleaned fresh corn, grilled or steamed
8 oz shredded Parmesan cheese

Mix all ingredients until blended. Place shredded Parmesan in shallow container. Roll hot corn in the garlic mayo dressing, cover them completely, then roll in shredded Parmesan.

Scallop and Apples with Maple Chili Buerre Blanc

CHEF WIL PELLY
Sanctuaria

8 – 10 scallops (large diver scallops)
1 Granny Smith apple, cored and sliced as thin as possible
1 Tbsp shallot, minced
1 oz. white wine
1 oz. maple syrup
2 tsp clarified butter or vegetable oil
2 Tbsp unsalted butter
salt and red pepper flakes to taste

Pat the scallops dry with a paper towel. Heat a nonstick skillet over high heat. Add clarified butter or oil. Season each scallop with a pinch of salt. Place them in the hot oil (just when pan begins to smoke).
After one minute flip the scallops over and cook for another minute. Remove the scallops and set aside. Pour off most of the butter or oil and add shallots. Cook for 30 seconds at medium heat. Deglaze with white wine. Add red pepper flakes and salt to taste. Add apple slices and cook for a few minutes until wine has almost evaporated Add syrup and cook for a minute or two till it gets tacky. Remove from heat and add the cold butter. Swirl the pan in a circular motion until butter has made a sauce.

Plate scallops and drizzle sauce over top.

Taste of Soulard

Bread Pudding with Whiskey Sauce (V)
Soulard's Restaurant

3 eggs
1 C sugar
1 ½ tsp cinnamon
½ tsp nutmeg
2 tsp vanilla extract
2-2 ½ C whole milk
4 medium peaches, peeled and sliced
4 medium apples, peeled and sliced
6 C of ½ inch cubed day old bread (Italian or French)
¼ stick of butter cut into cubes

Preheat oven to 350 degrees. In a large bowl, combine, eggs, sugar, cinnamon, nutmeg, vanilla and milk. Mix until well blended. Add fruit, then bread. Toss to be sure the bread has been mixed well in the liquid. Place in a greased 9" x13" pan. Top with butter and bake for 1 hour. Serve warm with whiskey sauce.

Whiskey Sauce Ingredients:
1 C whiskey
1 lb butter
2 C sugar

In a medium saucepan, whisk together all ingredients, and cook over medium heat until the sugar dissolves and sauce is hot.

La Festa

"St. Ambrose Roman Catholic Church is at the heart of the Hill, an Italian immigrant neighborhood in St. Louis. Their annual carnival, La Festa, is usually held on the first Sunday of May. La Festa begins after the Italian Mass at 11 am and continues until 6 pm. Sample Italian food specialties such as toasted ravioli, rice balls, mostaccioli with meatballs, cannoli and much more! St. Ambrose is located at 5130 Wilson Ave, 63110. Please visit their website at www.stambroseonthehill.com for more information."

Lena's Italian Meatballs

LAURA LAW
Pastoral Associate St. Ambrose Church

1 lb of lean ground chuck or sirloin
1 Tbsp of granulated garlic
½ C Italian seasoned bread crumbs
½ tsp red pepper flakes
salt and pepper to taste
½ C grated Parmesan cheese
1 egg
½ C warm water

Preheat oven to 350 degrees. Mix ingredients and form into 1 1/2 inch balls. Place on foil-lined cookie sheet lightly coated with non-stick cooking spray. Cook for 20 minutes. Add to hot spaghetti sauce and let simmer for twenty minutes. Mangia!

Stray Rescue – Yoga

ROMANIAN EthNiC festival

Every year on Columbus Day weekend St. Thomas the Apostle Romanian Orthodox Church (northeast corner of Francis Park in St. Louis Hills in the city) celebrates its Romanian heritage with a two-day festival. Founded by Romanian ethnics in 1935 as an off-shoot of St. Nicholas Greek Orthodox Church, its current membership boasts a significant number of post-1989 Romanian immigrants with a smattering of Albanian. The members spend the late summer preparing for the festival, most notably pickling cabbage leaves, a prime ingredient in sarmale (cabbage rolls). Not to be missed are the shish-kebobs and mici (homemade grilled sausages). Here are a couple of examples of homemade dishes guaranteed to be present on every Romanian table.

Salata De Vinate – Egg plant spread (V)

ADINA COVACI PRINCE

5 medium eggplants
4 Tbsp of vegetable oil
2 tsp of Dijon® mustard
2 egg yolks (one hard boiled and one raw)
1 minced medium white onion
½ tsp of salt
a clove of garlic

Choose 5 medium egg plants that are not too big nor too thick. Put them on a grill at a medium-high temperature and grill them on all the sides until the skin starts to break and the eggplant changes its usual firm aspect to a dryer, soft looking one. Place them in a colander in a sink to allow them to cool off and to let some of the liquid drain. After they have cooled off start peeling them under a very gentle stream of running water. After you peel each eggplant cut the stem off. Place the grilled eggplants on a cutting board and start mincing them with the wooden knife until they have the consistency of a paste. Place the eggplant paste in a bowl and using the wooden spoon start stirring until the paste becomes creamy. Separately, in a small bowl place the raw yolk and the boiled yolk and start beating them with a mixer while you add oil little by little until you obtain the quantity of mayonnaise that you wish to add for the quantity of the eggplant you have. Add salt, minced onion, and the clove of minced garlic and keep stirring to obtain a creamy and even mixture.

Serve the spread on slices of good quality bread. You can add pieces of green pepper and thin slices of tomatoes on top.

Ciorba de Perisoare – Sour Meatball Soup

ADINA COVACI PRINCE

1 lb ground meat (mixed beef and pork)
1 lb beef (or veal) with bones
2 small onions
2 slices of good bread
2 Tbsp rice
1 parsley root
3-4 carrots
1 parsnip root
3-4 Tbsp tomato paste
1 bunch of lovage leaves* (or parsley leaves)
2-3 Tbsp vinegar
salt and ground black pepper

* Lovage/lustean is a leafy herb used in cooking, teas, and folk remedies throughout Europe and parts of Asia. If not available in the local international markets parsley or celery leaves can be substituted.

Bring to boil 6 cups of water in a pot. Finely slice: 1 onion, the parsley, the parsnip and the carrots and put them in the water. Add the beef (or veal) meat. In the meantime soak the bread in water then squeeze it. Mash the bread with a fork. Mix the ground meat with the other finely chopped onion, the mashed bread and the rice, and season with salt and ground black pepper. For a more tender meat composition add 2-3 tablespoons of water. Make small meat balls rolling them with wet hands. When the vegetables become tender put the meat balls in the boiling water. Reduce heat and simmer for 30-40 minutes. When the soup is almost done the meatballs are coming to the surface as the soup simmers. Add the tomato paste and stir. Finely chop the lovage and add it to the soup, and then season with salt and vinegar. If you do not have lovage, you can use fresh parsley leaves instead. The soup is delicious served with a bit of sour cream, and a hot pepper on the side.

Chili

ANDY UECKER

1 quart cold water
2 lbs ground beef (use the leanest ground beef possible)
2 small cans tomato paste
2 yellow onions, diced
4 garlic cloves, minced
1 Tbsp Worcestershire® sauce
1 Tbsp unsweetened cocoa
¼ C chili powder
1 tsp cayenne
1 tsp ground cumin
2 Tbsp cider vinegar
1 whole bay leaf
¼ tsp ground cloves
1 tsp cinnamon
1½ tsp salt
Cooked spaghetti to serve chili over, optional

Add all the ingredients together except the beef. Bring to a slow simmer and start adding the beef in small amounts until all the beef falls apart in small pieces. Simmer on low, uncovered, for 3 hours. Add water as needed if the chili becomes too thick. 🦴

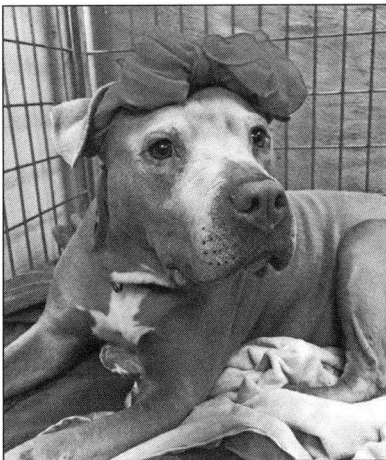

Stray Rescue – Crab Rangoon

"Recycled" Savory Bread Pudding (V)

COURTESY OF ST. LOUIS EARTH DAY'S PROGRAM,
Recycling On the Go.

This recipe is designed to use "recycled" or left-over items to create something amazing.

1 lb of crusty bread (left-over?)
1-2 cloves of garlic, minced
¼ C olive oil
2-3 Tbsp fresh thyme
3 oz butter
1 lb mushrooms (possibly foraged?)
1 large onion chopped
3 C chopped veggies – celery, bell pepper, zucchini (or use leftover veggies from dinner last night)
3½ C heavy cream
9 eggs
1 C grated cheese (Parmesan, aged cheddar, or anything with a sharp flavor)
salt and pepper to taste

Set oven to 375 degrees, and butter a 13" x 9" x 2" baking dish. Cube bread into 1 inch pieces and toss with olive oil, thyme, and garlic. Spread bread cubes on baking sheet, sprinkle with salt and pepper and bake for about 20 minutes until crispy. You may want to stir them once or twice while they crisp up. Reduce oven to 350 degrees. Put your crispy bread cubes into a large bowl. While bread cools, sauté mushrooms, onions and other veggies with the butter in a large skillet. Mix eggs and cream together.

Combine veggie mixture, bread cubes, and egg/cream mixture in a large bowl. Add mixture to the baking dish and sprinkle cheese over the top. Bake for about 1 hour at 350, uncovered, until top is golden. Allow to stand 15 minutes before serving. This may be prepared up to 1 day in advance and kept in the refrigerator before baking. The ingredients can be varied by what you have on hand. Try with different veggies, herbs and cheese combinations. Don't let anything go to waste!

Summer Pesto Pasta (V)
Green Dining Alliance

A program of St. Louis Earth Day,

This recipe is designed to use your bounty of fresh basil in the summer to create a tasty versatile sauce that is also vegan and gluten free.

1 lb of pasta (choose a fresh locally produced pasta for BEST results)
2 C of Basil leaves
1 C extra virgin olive oil
4-5 cloves of garlic, minced
½ C pine nuts (or any other nuts you enjoy)
½ C of nutritional yeast (for vegan recipe, but you may use Parmesan cheese if you prefer)

Prepare pasta according to cooking directions. Puree basil leaves, olive oil, garlic, nuts and nutritional yeast in a food processor until a bright green shiny pesto sauce forms. Toss cooked pasta with pesto sauce. For a variation, try adding tomatoes (either sun-dried or fresh-peeled), olives, or steamed veggies. Extra sauce can be frozen and used at a later time. It is also great as a sandwich spread.

Crisp Kale, Sweet Potato, Quinoa Cakes (V)

ST. LOUIS EARTH DAY

This recipe is designed to use garden items either in early spring, or fall.

2½ C cooked quinoa
1 medium onion, diced
2-3 Tbsp olive oil
4-5 cloves of garlic, minced
2 C shredded sweet potato
3 C de-stemmed, chopped kale
4 oz. tomato paste
3 eggs
⅓ C flour (may substitute Gluten Free flour)
2 Tbsp flax seeds, ground, mixed with 6 tbsp. warm water
½ C fresh oregano leaves, chopped (may substitute 2 tbsp. dry)
salt and pepper to taste

Set oven to 400 degrees. Sauté onion, garlic and shredded sweet potato in skillet for about 5 minutes. Add kale and continue to sauté for another 5 minutes. Allow mixture to cool a bit and add to the quinoa. Mix in the remaining ingredients. Form into patties with about ½ cup of mixture and place on baking sheet. Bake for 15 minutes, flip the patties and bake for another 15 minutes. Serve with your favorite sauce. Great with remoulade. These are hearty enough to be a main dish, but would also make a great appetizer or side dish. We picked kale and oregano from the spring garden for this recipe. Sweet potatoes, onions, tomato paste and garlic were in storage from last season.

LOCAL MARKETS

Bruschetta Burgers
DIERBERG'S SCHOOL OF COOKING

1 carton (12 ounces) miniature heirloom tomatoes
¼ C chopped onion
1½ tsp chopped fresh basil
1½ tsp balsamic vinegar
1 tsp Dierbergs olive oil
2 tsp Montreal® steak seasoning
4 Dierbergs ground beef patties (about 1/3 pound each)
4 slices Dierbergs provolone cheese
4 slices french bread
1 avocado, halved, pitted, peeled, and sliced

In medium bowl, stir together tomatoes, onion, basil, vinegar, and olive oil until well mixed. Cover and chill 1 to 2 hours to develop flavors. Season both sides of burgers with steak seasoning. Place burgers on oiled grid over medium heat; cover and grill until internal temperature is 160°F., about 5 to 6 minutes per side. Place 1 slice cheese on each burger. Brush both sides of bread with olive oil. Place on grid over medium heat; grill until lightly charred. Place 1 burger on each bread slice; top with tomato mixture and avocado slices. Makes 4 servings.

Salted Caramel Ice Cream Pie (V)
DIERBERG'S SCHOOL OF COOKING

1 box (9 ounces) chocolate-covered pretzels (divided) (Dierbergs Produce Department)
3 Tbsp Dierbergs butter, melted and slightly cooled
½ gallon Dierbergs vanilla ice cream
⅔ C caramel ice cream topping
¾ tsp coarse salt

Reserve 8 pretzels for garnish. Place remaining pretzels in work bowl of food processor fitted with steel knife blade; process until finely chopped (about 1¾ cups). Add butter; pulse until crumbs hold together. Press mixture evenly onto bottom and up sides of 9-inch deep-dish pie plate. Freeze until set, about 20 minutes. Scoop two-thirds of the ice cream into balls and arrange in prepared pie crust; press and swirl with back of spoon. Microwave caramel topping in 15 second intervals until pourable consistency. Drizzle half of the caramel topping over ice cream. Repeat layers with remaining ice cream and topping. Freeze until firm, at least 4 hours. Let pie stand at room temperature 10 minutes. Cut into wedges, sprinkle salt over top, and garnish with reserved pretzels.

Makes 8 servings.

Pot Roast with Fingerling Potatoes
STRAUB'S MARKETS

3 lbs Eye of Round roast
1 yellow onion—roughly chopped
4 cloves garlic—peeled
1 C red wine
3 C beef broth
2 Tbsp tomato paste

In an herb sachet:
1 bay leaf
1 sprig fresh rosemary
4 sprigs fresh thyme
14 oz assorted fingerling potatoes—split in half length-wise
6 oz baby carrots
10 oz parsnips—peeled & cut on a bias

Preheat oven to 325°F. Liberally season the beef with salt & pepper. Heat a braising pan over high heat & add oil. Place the beef roast in the pan, browning the meat on both sides (approx. 4-5 minutes per side). Remove the roast and set it aside. Add chopped onion and garlic to the hot pan. Sauté until the onions start to brown. Deglaze the pan with the red wine and allow it to reduce until almost dry. Add beef broth & tomato paste, bringing the sauce to a boil. Add the reserved beef roast & the sachet of herbs. Cover with a tightly fitted lid & bake at 325F for approx. 2 ½ hours or until tender.*

Check the meat by slicing off a piece. Thickness of the cut may cause baking times to vary.
Add potatoes, carrots & parsnips. Bake for an additional 25 minutes.

Remove from the oven & serve.

Michelle's Dressy Black Beans (V)
CITY GREENS MARKET

1 container frozen del Carmen Cuban Style Black Beans®
½ C plain Greek Windcrest Dairy Yogurt®
2 C uncooked MaKaskles Family Farm Rice® -brown
¼ C grated Marcoot Jersey Creamery White Cheddar Cheese®
2 tomatoes
1 tsp cilantro, finely chopped (optional)

Cook rice according to package directions, keeping in mind that brown rice cooks for longer than white rice. Heat black beans on stovetop or in microwave until hot, stirring constantly. While rice and beans are cooking, grate cheese and dice tomato. When beans and rice are done, put 1/2 cup cooked rice in the bottom of a bowl. Add 1/2 cup beans. Add 1/4 cup yogurt. Add diced tomato. Sprinkle with cheese and cilantro.

Grilled Caesar Salad (V)

DIERBERGS SCHOOL OF COOKING

1 bag (12 to 16 ounces) romaine hearts
Dierbergs extra virgin olive oil
3 lemons, halved
½ tsp coarse salt
Freshly ground black pepper
1 C Caesar-style croutons
½ C shaved Parmesan cheese

Rinse lettuce and pat dry. Slice each in half lengthwise, leaving root end intact. Generously brush cut surfaces with olive oil. Place cut-sides down on oiled grid over medium-high heat; grill turning once until leaves are lightly charred, about 2-3 minutes. Brush cut-sides of lemons with olive oil. Place lemons cut-sides down on oiled grid over medium-high heat; grill until lightly charred and grill marks appear, about 2 to 3 minutes. Place romaine wedges on 6 individual serving plates. Squeeze grilled lemon halves over tops; season with salt and pepper. Sprinkle croutons and cheese over tops. Serve immediately.

Heirloom Tomato Tart (V)

DIERBERGS SCHOOL OF COOKING

1 refrigerated pie crust (½ of 14.1 ounce package)
1 lb heirloom or homegrown tomatoes, thinly sliced (about 3 medium)
1 container (8 oz) Dierbergs Deli provel cheese ropes
2 tsp McCormick Greek Seasoning® (divided)

Unroll pie crust onto lightly floured surface. Roll dough lightly into 12-inch circle. Fit into 9-inch tart pan with removable bottom. Press dough against sides of pan; trim off excess dough. Pierce bottom with tines of fork. Bake in 450°F oven until lightly browned, about 8 minutes; cool slightly. Reduce oven temperature to 375°F. Place tomato slices on paper towels to remove excess moisture. Arrange ¾ of the cheese over crust; top with tomatoes, 1 teaspoon of the seasoning, remaining cheese, and remaining 1 teaspoon seasoning. Bake until cheese melts and begins to brown, about 20 to 22 minutes. Let stand 5 minutes; remove ring from pan and cut into wedges. Makes 6 servings.

FOOD TRUCKS

The Famous Naancho

TIKKA TIKKA TACO FOOD TRUCK

2 lb boneless skinless chicken breast
1 Tbsp garlic-ginger paste
2 tsp softened butter (optional)
1 Packet T3 Tikka Spice Mix®
1 Tbsp lemon juice
¼ C plain yogurt (for marinade)
1 C plain yogurt (for raita)
1 bunch cilantro, chopped to about ½ cup
1 packet T3 Raita Spice Mix®
1 tsp minced garlic (optional)
*4 C baby spinach (1 (10 oz) bag will be enough)**
½ C diced pickled jalapeños
1 C crumbled feta cheese

At LEAST an hour before grilling prepare the chicken. Cut chicken into bite size thick strips. This enough to get as much spice coverage as possible but thick enough to grill. Put in a medium size bowl. Mix in Butter, Garlic Ginger Paste, and Lemon Juice. Coat chicken. Mix in Packet of T3 Tikka Spice Mix. Coat chicken. Marinade overnight if possible, but at least an 90 min prior to grilling, mix in ¼ Cup Plain Yogurt. Once again, coat chicken. After mixing in the yogurt, leave chicken at room temperature until you grill. Put the 1 Cup yogurt in a bowl, and mix in the 1 Packet T3 Raita Spice Mix and half of your cilantro (¼ cup). Mix VERY thoroughly. Preheat oven at 400 degrees.

At that point, decide whether you want to create a self-serve assembly line for the Naanchos, or plate them yourself. If doing an assembly line, place the following in separate dishes/bowls with spoons or tongs: the Raita you just made above, spinach, feta, jalapeños and the rest of the cilantro for garnish.

Grill the chicken! Be careful not to dry out the thin strips, but of course, make sure you cook through.

Once the chicken is on the grill, toast 4-6 pieces of naan at 400 degrees. Once it is to your liking, cut it into large 'chip' size pieces, and put in a bowl/tray. When the chicken is done, cube it into bite size pieces, and add it to the line! On a plate or a 3 lb Paper Fry Tray, assemble your dish in this suggested order: Lay down a layer naan chips, grab a handful (or tong-full) of spinach and layer over top. Throw on about a ⅓ lb of chicken Drizzle about a 1½ TBSP of Raita. Top with feta, jalapeños and cilantro to taste! You can really use any greens you want, but I like either spinach or a 50/50 blend of Spinach and Spring Mix or Kale.

Our Grilled Cheese (V)

2 GIRLS 4 WHEELS FOOD TRUCK

2 pieces of Texas toast
2 thick cut pieces of muenster cheese
1 broken slice of Colby Jack cheese
1 pitted date cut into 5 pieces
1 Tbsp garlic (adjust to your liking)
¼ tsp cayenne pepper (adjust to your liking)
1 Tbsp butter, softened
1 C mayonnaise
Side of marinara sauce for dipping

Make your spread by combining butter, mayonnaise, garlic and cayenne pepper. Spread mixture on the outside of the bread. Place one slice of bread, butter side down on a Panini press (can also grill if desired). Assemble the cheese and place the date onto the bread on all corners and the middle. Place the remaining slice of bread with butter side out. Grill and serve with a side of marinara sauce for dipping.

StlouisianaQ Jambalaya

STLOUISIANQ FOOD TRUCK

½ lb Andouille sausage
½ lb chicken cooked and shredded
2 lb shrimp cooked and deveined

Louisiana Holy Trinity
2 celery ribs chopped, 1 large onion chopped, 1 medium green pepper chopped
¼ C oil
5 green onions chopped
2 garlic cloves minced
4 large tomatoes diced
1 tsp thyme
1 tsp salt
1 tsp pepper
½ tsp wayenne wepper
28 ounces chicken broth
1 C uncooked long grain rice
⅓ C water

Sauté sausage in oil until lightly browned. Remove and set aside. Sauté the Louisiana Holy Trinity and green onions until tender. Add garlic and cook 1 minute longer. Stir in tomatoes, thyme, salt, pepper and cayenne pepper, cook 5 minutes longer. Stir in broth, rice and water. Bring to a boil. Reduce heat and cover. Simmer for 20 minutes or until rice is tender. Stir in andouille sausage, chicken and shrimp. Heat through.

FiSH FRY'S

Father Jack's Salmon
ST. MARY MAGDALANE PARISH

4 (8oz.) Icelandic salmon fillets
Olive Oil or butter
Equal parts granulated garlic, salt and butter

Directions: Brush each fillet with olive oil or butter. Sprinkle with equal parts granulated garlic, salt & pepper

Cucumber Dill Sauce
1 cucumber, peeled and seeded - cut into chunks
1 C of sour cream
1 C of mayonnaise
2 Tbsp fresh lemon juice
1-2 garlic cloves minced
1 tsp Salt
⅔ C fresh Dill

Dust each salmon fillet with garlic, salt and pepper. Bake at 350° for 20-25 minutes.

To prepare Cucumber Dill Sauce – put peeled and seeded cucumber chunks in food processor. Pulse until smooth. Try to drain some of the water off of the cucumber so the sauce is not runny. Add sour cream, mayonnaise, lemon juice, minced garlic, salt and dill into processor with cucumber and blend until smooth.

Baked Sole
ST. MARY MAGDALANE PARISH

4 (8 oz.) Swai fillets (we use Swai fish because it is less fishy)
¼ C lemon juice mixed with a ¼ up cooking sherry
2 tsp granulated garlic
2 tsp salt
2 tsp pepper

Lay out fish fillets on rimmed cookie sheet on parchment paper. Mix lemon juice and Sherry in a cup and pour over the fillets. Mix granulated garlic, salt and pepper in a small cup and then sprinkle this seasoning mixture over each fillet.

Bake fish at 350° for 20 minutes and serve with a fresh lemon wedge.

Sacred Heart Slaw Recipe (V)

MOST SACRED HEART PARISH EUREKA, MO

3 lbs shredded Cabbage
2 medium carrots, grated
1 small white onion, chopped
2 ribs of celery, chopped
½ bell pepper, diced
¼ tsp celery salt
Salt and pepper to taste

Put all ingredients on top of the cabbage in a large bowl. Toss in the dressing. Recipe below.

Cole Slaw Dressing
1½ C sugar
1 C apple cider vinegar
½ C of Crisco Oil

Mix all ingredients together with a hand mixer. Pour over the cabbage and vegetables and combine about 45 minutes before serving.

Stray Rescue – Heparin

FARMERS MARKETS

Cream Cheese Spread (V)

LAURA BOZZAY
Adventures In Spice, LLC on behalf of Ferguson Farmer's Market

8 oz package of cream cheese (no fat works well)
1 Tbsp of any of the following: Sultan's Blend® (no salt, no sugar, no additives),
Mediterranean Dreams®, Insanity Ridge®, Spicy Cajun® (no salt, no sugar, no additives),
Venetian Twilight®, Tagine® (no salt, no sugar, no additives), Riviera Onion Pepper ®(no salt) or Spanish Seafood and
Rice® (no salt, no sugar, no additives)

Mix well, serve cold.

"I Love to Eat Greens" Locavore Superfood Raw Kale Salad (V)

MOLLY ROCKAMANN
EarthDance Organic Farm School on behalf of Ferguson Farmer's Market

2 bunches of curly leaf kale* (purple and green mixed makes for a colorful salad!), de-stemmed and torn
  into bite-size pieces
½ red onion, sliced thinly
3 – 4 carrots, shredded
1 pint blueberries, fresh
½ C pecans, whole or pieces
Add other chopped fresh veggies or fruits or nuts as in season and available!

Dressing
Juice of 3-4 large lemons
½ C olive oil
a few squirts of Bragg's Amino Acids® (or soy sauce)
1 Tbsp of tahini (sesame seed paste)
1 garlic glove*
½ inch fresh ginger root*
1 Tbsp of local honey
  ** to sweeten a bit, if desired.

Blend all dressing ingredients in a blender (or Magic Bullet-type appliance) until creamy. If no blender is available, mince the garlic and ginger finely and shake all ingredients together in a jar.

Toss the salad in the dressing. Tastes best the next day! (I often make twice as much and keep it on hand in my fridge so that I always have something healthy and delicious ready-made at home!)

Stuffed Mushrooms (V)

LAURA BOZZAY
Adventures In Spice, LLC on behalf of Ferguson Farmer's Market

1½ lbs mushrooms (about 20 full mushrooms)
1 Tbsp Naples Robusto®
10 oz package frozen spinach
¼ C dry bread crumbs
1 Tbsp margarine or butter

Clean mushrooms and remove stem. Set mushroom caps aside. Combine all ingredients. Fill caps with ingredients. Serve warm or cold. To serve warm, place in oven for about 5 minutes at 350.

Option, substitute cream cheese for butter.

Cream Cheese Cookies (V)

LAURA BOZZAY
Adventures In Spice, LLC on behalf of Ferguson Farmer's Market

8 oz of cream cheese
1 C shortening
1 C Vanilla Sugar
1 C flour
1 egg

Preheat oven to 375. Cream together cream cheese, shortening, and vanilla sugar. Add in one egg and beat on high for about 2 minutes. Fold in flour. Drop by baby spoon or small teaspoon onto aluminum foil lined cookie sheet. Bake about 8 to 10 minutes or until top is not wet looking and edges are slightly tan. Cool on wire rack.

Multigrain Blueberry Pancakes (V)

Ellisville Farmer's Market

2 C fresh blueberries or frozen that have been thawed and drained; other seasonal fruit is also an option
   (strawberries, peaches, pears and apples are also good)
2 C purpose flour (about)
1 Tbsp baking powder
1 tsp baking soda
1 tsp salt
Sift all these together in mixing bowl
Add about ⅔ C uncooked rolled oats (old fashion oatmeal, not quick cooking or instant)
3 Tbsp sugar
Stir in
1½ C milk or buttermilk (put 1 Tbsp white vinegar into milk and let it set a while to make buttermilk)
2 large eggs- mixed into milk
½ stick (4 Tbsp) butter melted and stirred into milk
2 Tbsp vegetable oil also mixed in

Pour all of the above into flour mixture and stir. If it is too thick add a little more milk- tiny bit at a time- if it's too thin, whisk in a little more flour. On a hot griddle, pour out individual pancakes. When they get a little dry around the edges and bubbly in the center, put blueberries into the tops and press them in a little. Then flip and cook a little longer. Serve with more blueberries on the top.

Stray Rescue – Alex Steen

Crepes with Goat Cheese and Strawberry Sauce (V)

RYAN MAHER
Webster Groves Farmers Market

Crepe Batter
1½ C all purpose flour
2 C whole milk
3 eggs
¼ C butter, melted
Pinch of kosher or sea salt

Strawberry Sauce
½ lb fresh strawberries
2 Tbsp granulated cane sugar
½ C water
Dash of vanilla extract
Small pinch of salt

Goat Cheese Mousse
½ lb fresh goat cheese (plain)
¼ C whole milk
2 Tbsp honey
Zest and juice of one lemon
1 tsp kosher or sea salt

To make the crepes: Pour the milk into a blender then add the eggs, flour and salt. On low speed, blend until smooth. Slowly add the melted butter and run for another minute or so. Refrigerate for one hour. Heat a non-stick pan over medium high heat for a few minutes then spray with non-stick cooking spray. Ladle in enough batter to just barely cover the pan, then slowly swirl the batter to the edges. Cook for about a minute until the crepe releases from the pan. Flip and cook for another thirty seconds or so. The batter or the heat may need to be adjusted as the first crepe rarely comes out perfect. Batter should be half as thick as pancake batter. Crepes can be made a day in advance and warmed slightly in the microwave or oven prior to use but are best if made just before filling.

To make the strawberry sauce: Cut the strawberries thinly and place into a saucepan that is at least three times the volume of your sauce (to prevent a messy boil over.) Add the remaining ingredients and bring to a boil. Reduce heat and simmer for five minutes. Serve hot, cold or at room temperature. Sauce can be made ahead of time and refrigerated for up to a week or frozen for six months.

To make the goat cheese mousse: It is best to use a stand mixer with the paddle attachment but a food processor or mixing bowl and rubber spatula will work as well. Combine all of the mousse ingredients and mix until smooth. This can be done ahead of time but should be brought to room temperature before serving.

To finish the crepes: Place a crepe on a flat surface. Spoon some of the mousse onto one quarter of the crepe and fold the crepe onto it making a half moon then fold it one more time to create the triangle. Finish with the strawberry sauce and enjoy! Fresh mint is a tasty garnish.

Farmer's Market Fall Roasted Spicy Squash Soup

Wildwood Farmer's Market

One large winter squash
Olive oil
Kosher salt and fresh ground black pepper
1-1½ C of yellow onion diced
2 ribs Chopped celery
1 C diced carrots
2 cloves chopped garlic- be careful not to burn
2-3 slices of bacon (optional)
1 tsp ground cinnamon
1 tsp ground cumin
Pinch of allspice
1 tsp of curry powder
½ tsp of ground ginger
Kosher salt and fresh ground pepper to taste

Preheat oven to 400 degrees. Cut the squash through the lobes (be very careful) and clean off the seeds. Grease a large baking sheet with olive oil. Place the squash on the baking sheet and brush each piece with olive oil and sprinkle with kosher salt and fresh ground pepper. Roast the pan of squash until tender and browned. Let cool and carefully cut the squash from the rind and cut into large chunks

While the squash is roasting, Sauté the following in olive oil in large skillet or stock pot. When veggies are soft, add the chunks of squash and mash together. Add spices and seasonings to taste Add milk and/or cream, stir in. Put mixture in blender to puree or mash thoroughly with potato masher and hand mixer. Add more milk and/or cream to the desired thickness, adjust seasonings and heat through.

Soulard Gooey Butter Cake (V)

SCOTT SCHWEIGER
Soulard Farmer's Market

½ C butter, (ONLY REAL BUTTER!)
18 ounces yellow cake mix (usually one box)
3 eggs
1 (8 oz) package cream cheese (cut into 4 parts)
½ tsp pure vanilla extract
4 C Powdered sugar

Preheat oven to 350. Lightly grease (or spray) one deep 9" x13" rectangular cake pan. I would suggest a 4 inch deep pan, as the cake rises when it is cooking. But an oven-safe disposable coffee cake pan from the store would work as well. Melt the butter in microwave on low power for 30 seconds.

Empty cake mix into a large bowl. Stir melted butter, along with ONE egg, into the cake mix. PRESS the mixture into pan. Mixture will have the consistency of sticky dough. Using a spatula works well, but pressing with clean fingers will do the trick as well. In a large bowl, mix cream cheese, vanilla extract, powdered sugar and the remaining two eggs. Beat for three minutes with an electric mixer set on medium high speed, or until smooth, leave no lumps. Pour evenly over top of the cake mixture in the pan. Use a spatula to spread. Place a large cookie sheet or foil on the rack below the cake in case the cake bubbles over. The cookie sheet or foil will save you from a big clean-up.

Bake at 350 for 30-45 minutes until golden brown on top. Cooking time is estimated, you will really have to watch it here! I always take the cake out when it turns a darkish golden brown. Note that there will be a paper thin sugar "crust" that will form while the cake is baking. It the top layer of sugar hardening, and this is what will turn golden brown. Allow cake to cool. This is very important, as the cake will not cut easily until it is completely cool. The cake will sink in as it sets up. This is normal. Sprinkle the top with powdered sugar.

Cut the cake into squares and serve with milk and plenty of napkins, it can be messy but very enjoyable.

*This isn't credited to anyone in particular but it's a great recipe. I have used in the past but it has no author or creator as far as I know, It was scribbled down on an old piece of lined paper and given to me years ago.

FRieNDS ReCiPeS

FRIENDS BREAKFAST, BREADS AND MUFFINS

Josephine's Famous Cheese Filled Bacon Muffins

MARIANNE JUNGER, STAFF AT STRAY RESCUE

1 lb bacon, drained and crumbled (save 1/2 C grease)
1½ C pancake mix
½ C milk
1 egg
⅓ C onion, chopped
2 oz. American cheese, cut into 12 half-inch cubes

Grease muffin cups or line with paper cups. In large bowl, combine pancake mix, milk, reserved bacon grease and egg. By hand, stir until blended. Add bacon and onion; stir until blended. Spoon batter into muffin cups, filling ⅔ full. Press a cheese cube in center of batter. Bake at 425 degrees for 15-20 minutes or until golden brown.

Pumpkin Bread (V)

SUE WOODS

3⅓ C flour
2 tsp baking soda
3 C sugar
1 tsp salt
4 eggs
1 (15 oz) can pumpkin
1 C vegetable oil
1 C raisins
3 tsp cinnamon
1 C chopped nuts
2 tsp nutmeg

Cream sugar and eggs together. Add oil, flour, cinnamon, nutmeg, soda, salt and pumpkin. Add raisins and nuts. Pour in greased and floured loaf pans half full. Bake 350 degrees for about 30 minutes.

Cole Breakfast Cake (V)

SUSAN FARRIS

Cake Ingredients:
1 box yellow cake mix
1 box large vanilla instant pudding
½ C canola oil
1 C water
4 eggs
1 tsp vanilla

Toppings:
1 C sugar
2 tsp cinnamon
1 C pecans
1 C raisins
Chocolate chips, optional

Preheat oven to 350 degrees. Mix cake ingredients together well and beat 3-5 minutes. Place half of the batter into a 9" x 13" greased pan. Mix topping ingredients together well. Sprinkle half of the topping mix over the batter. Pour the other half of batter in pan and put the remaining topping on the batter. Swirl with table knife through batter. Bake for 45 minutes. Top will be golden brown.

Butterscotch Rolls (V)

LAVONNE STEVENSON, FOREST LAKE, MN

36 frozen dinner rolls or 2 loaves of frozen bread dough, cut into 1" slices
1 C pecans or walnuts, chopped
3 oz pkg butterscotch pudding (not instant)
1 C brown sugar
½ C butter, melted

Thaw bread dough in refrigerator overnight. Spray a 9" x 13" baking dish with non-stick cooking spray. Sprinkle chopped nuts in bottom of pan. Place dough over nuts. Sprinkle with pudding and brown sugar. Melt butter and pour over dough. Let rise until it doubles in size. Bake in a 350 degree oven for 20-25 minutes. Turn out onto baking sheet or plate.

Cinnamon Raisin Bread French Toast Soufflé (V)

ALICIA MINER

2 loaves raisin bread, cubed
12 oz cream cheese, softened (1½ boxes)
1½ sticks butter, softened
¾ C maple syrup
10 eggs
3 C half and half
2 Tbsp sugar and 1 Tbsp cinnamon, mixed together
2 Tbsp powdered sugar

Place cubed bread in well-greased casserole dish, preferably glass. Mix cream cheese, butter and ¼ cup syrup until smooth. Beat eggs, half and half, ½ cup syrup. Pour egg mixture over the bread. Top with cream cheese mixture. Sprinkle with cinnamon and sugar. Cover and refrigerate overnight. Uncover and bake at 350 degrees for 50-55 minutes. Sprinkle with powdered sugar and serve with buttered syrup.

Buttered syrup: mix 50/50 ratio of syrup to butter. Heat until butter is melted and mix well.

Cream Cheese Danish (V)

SARAH DENEAU, VOLUNTEER, ADOPTER, FOSTER

2 (8 oz) packages cream cheese, softened
2 (8 oz) crescent rolls
⅔ C sugar
1 tsp vanilla
2 eggs

Grease a 9" x 13" pan and preheat oven to 350 degrees. Press one can of rolls on bottom of pan. Mix cream cheese, sugar, vanilla and one egg together. Blend until smooth. Spread on top of crescent roll layer. Press other can of rolls onto waxed paper, then place on top of filling, removing waxed paper. Beat egg and brush on top of crescent roll. Bake 20-25 minutes until gold brown.

Snickerdoodle Bread (V)

TRACEY HAMMACK

2½ C flour
1 tsp baking powder
½ tsp salt
2 tsp cinnamon
1 C butter, softened
2 C sugar
3 eggs
1 tsp vanilla
¾ C regular or light sour cream
1 pkg. Hershey's cinnamon chips
3 Tbsp sugar
3 tsp cinnamon

Preheat oven to 350 degrees. Cream butter, sugar, salt, and cinnamon until fluffy. Add eggs and mix well. Add vanilla and sour cream until mixed well. Mix flour and baking powder in a separate bowl. Add to wet ingredients and mix until well combined. Add cinnamon chips and stir into batter. Spoon batter into 4 mini loaf pans until about ⅔ full. Mix 3 tbsp. sugar and 3 tsp. cinnamon in a small bowl and sprinkle over the batter in each loaf pan. Bake at 350 degrees for 35-.38 minutes. Let cool before removing from pan.

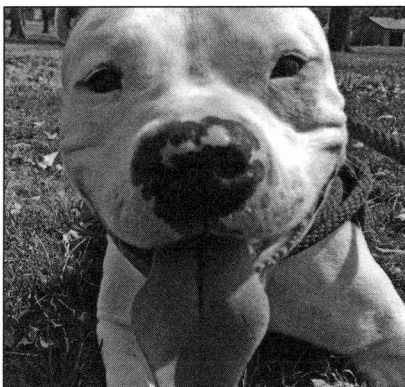

Stray Rescue – Angel Muffin

Dutch Baby (V)

SARAH DENEAU, VOLUNTEER, ADOPTER, FOSTER

3 Tbsp butter, melted and divided
½ C all purpose flour
3 Tbsp powdered sugar, plus extra for serving
½ tsp kosher salt
½ C whole milk, room temperature
2 large eggs, room temperature
Lemon wedges

Preheat oven to 375 degrees. Place 2 tablespoons of melted butter into a 10" cast iron skillet and place in the oven. Set the remaining tablespoon of melted butter aside to cool slightly. Wait 10 minutes before assembling the other ingredients. Place the flour, powdered sugar, salt, milk, eggs and remaining tablespoon of melted butter into the bowl of a food processor and process for 30 seconds. Carefully pour the batter into the preheated skillet. Bake on the middle rack of the oven for 30 to 35 minutes or until the edges are puffed and brown. Before serving, sprinkle with additional powdered sugar and lemon juice.

Crustless Mini Quiches

MARY THIESSEN

Nonstick cooking spray
3 green onions, finely diced
1 tomato, diced
4 slices of bacon, cooked and crumbled
6 large eggs
⅔ C whole milk
⅔ C heavy cream
1 tsp kosher salt
½ tsp ground black pepper
¾ C shredded sharp Cheddar cheese

Preheat the oven to 375 degrees. Lightly spray two 24-cup mini muffin pans or line with paper liners. Cook 4 slices of bacon. Crumble when cooled. While cooking the bacon, dice tomato and green onions. In a bowl, whisk together eggs, milk, cream, salt and pepper. Stir in bacon, onions and tomato, then stir in cheddar cheese. Transfer to a large glass measuring pitcher. Place the prepared muffin pans on 1 or 2 rimmed baking sheets to catch any drips. Add a few small pieces of broccoli and a generous pinch of cheese to each of the cups. Pour the egg mixture in each cup, filling as many as you can to just below the rim. Bake until the tops are puffed and just beginning to brown, about 15 minutes. Transfer to wire racks and let cool for about 5 minutes

Note: Can substitute half of a head of broccoli, chopped and pre-cooked, in place of the onion and tomato.
I often freeze these in a Ziploc bag and then on days when the kids and I are in a hurry, we just pop 1-2 in the microwave for 60-90 seconds and we have an instant breakfast.

Karen's Waffles (V)

SUE SCHALK

4 C flour
¼ C sugar
1½ tsp baking powder
½ tsp salt
3¾ C milk
1½ C oil
½ tsp vanilla
6 eggs

Heat waffle iron, and spray with non-stick cooking spray. Mix all ingredients in blender until mixed well and pour onto hot waffle iron. Cook according to waffle iron directions. Serve warm with desired toppings.

Mocha Protein Smoothie (V)

MARY HEMME

1 C coffee (cold)
1 scoop of protein powder of your choice (chocolate or vanilla)
2 Tbsp unsweetened Vanilla Almond Milk (or soy, cashew or coconut)
2 Tbsp unsweetened Cocoa
One frozen banana

Dump the cold coffee in blender over one scoop of vanilla protein and two tablespoons of cocoa, a frozen banana and splash of almond milk. Then blend, add more or less almond milk to get it to the consistency you like.

Pumpkin Chocolate Chip Spice Muffins (V)

MARY HEMME

1 box spice cake mix
1 (15 oz.) can pure pumpkin puree
½ C mini semi-sweet chocolate chips

Preheat oven to 350 F. Combine all ingredients in a medium bowl. Grease a 12 cup muffin tin or line with paper wrappers. Scoop the batter into the muffin tins. Bake for 18-22 minutes, until a toothpick inserted in the center comes out clean.

Glazed Raspberry Cheese Pie (V)

KAREN GISSY

2 C cheddar cheese, shredded
2 C provel cheese, shredded
1 bunch green onions, chopped
1 C pecans, chopped
4 – 5 Tbsp mayonnaise
10 oz jar of seedless raspberry preserves

Line a 9" pie plate with plastic wrap, leaving a large overhang. Mix all ingredients except preserves. Press into pie plate and fold plastic wrap over to cover. Chill well. When ready to serve, invert onto a serving plate and remove plastic wrap. Frost top and sides with raspberry preserves. Serve with crackers. 🦴

Cheese Ball

DIANE KALLAL

1 (8 oz) pkg cream cheese, softened
1 (5 oz) jar/blue lid Old English® cheddar cheese
1 (5 oz) jar pimento cheese
1 (5 oz) jar Roka® cheese
1 C cheddar/mozzarella cheese shreds
1 (2.5 oz) jar (Hormel®) dried beef, cut small
2 green onions, sliced
2 C pecans, chopped

Mix all ingredients, except pecans. Put 1 1/2 cups pecans in bottom of a medium bowl. Put cheese mixture in bowl and top with more chopped pecans. Keep refrigerated until serving. 🦴

Zesty Cheese Dip Recipe

MINDY SUE SHIRLEY

1 lb block Velveeta®, cubed
8 oz cream cheese, cubed
One (14.5 oz) can Rotel®
One (10.75 oz) can of cream of mushroom soup
1 lb of sausage, fried

Combine first four ingredients in crock pot on low. Once cheese is melted, add in the sausage. Serve with tortilla chips, veggies, etc. 🦴

Pecan Teasers (V)

MARY WHITEAKER

⅓ C bacon bits*
½ C pecans, chopped
1 C cheddar cheese, shredded
1 tsp onion, grated
½ C mayonnaise
¼ – ½ tsp salt, to taste
12 slices thin, white bread

Remove crusts from bread. Cut each slice into 4 triangles. Combine all other ingredients and spread on bread triangles. Bake at 350 degrees until lightly brown. Serve warm. 🦴

* MCCormack Bacon Bits® and Betty Crocker Bacos® are vegan. If using bacon this reipe is not vegetarian.

Hummus with Feta (V)

SALLY B. SIMPSON, STRAY RESCUE VOLUNTEER

1 (10 oz) Tub classic hummus
Crumbled Feta cheese
Cucumber
Tomato

Spread hummus in shallow dish and sprinkle with crumbled feta cheese. Top off with 1/4 cup fresh cucumber and 1/4 cup freshly chopped tomato. Serve with crackers. 🦴

Enrapturing Arugula Salad (V)

SARAH DAS

Arugula
1 medium onion, cut into slivers
2 C sharp cheddar cheese
2 C pecans, to taste

Dressing
1 Tbsp cashew butter
1 Tbsp olive oil, more if needed
1 lemon, juiced
1 clove garlic
Freshly ground black pepper, generous amount
Pinch of salt

Roast pecans and set aside to cool. Prepare dressing by mixing cashew butter, olive oil, lemon juice, finely minced garlic, salt and pepper. Coat arugula and onions in a serving bowl. Add slices of cheddar cheese and pecans. Top off with more freshly ground black pepper.

This is a nice healthy creamy salad base, delicious as is, or you may wish to add other complimentary toppings.

Versatile Snack Mix

PEGGY ROPPOLO

4 C Bugles®
4 C cheese crackers
1 C bagel chips
¼ C peanuts
1 Tbsp toasted sesame seeds
1½ Tbsp vegetable oil
½ Tbsp Worcestershire® sauce
1 tsp onion powder
1 tsp garlic powder

Preheat oven to 200 degrees. Spread first 4 ingredients evenly in roasting pan, in a small frying pan, slowly toast sesame seeds over medium heat until golden brown. Remove from heat and stir in the oil, Worcestershire sauce, onion powder and garlic powder. Drizzle mixture over dry ingredients. Mix to evenly coat snack mix. Bake for 10 minutes. Stir and bake for another 10 minutes. Note: keep an eye on snack mix to prevent scorching or burning. Spread mixture on a towel or wax paper to cool. When cool, store in an airtight container.

Variations: substitute any type of unsweetened, crunchy cereal or snack for any or all of the first 3 ingredients. Substitute mixed nuts or almonds for the peanuts.

Baked Egg Rolls (V)
DEE RAY

1 Tbsp cornstarch
2 Tbsp low-sodium soy sauce
1 tsp sugar
1 Tbsp canola oil
1 (12-14 oz) bag coleslaw mix (about 5 cups)
½ C water chestnuts, finely chopped
2 small scallions, finely chopped
2 cloves garlic
1 (14 oz) package extra-firm tofu, drained and cut into 1/4 inch dice
16 egg roll wrappers

Preheat oven to 425 degrees. Mist a baking sheet with cooking spray. Whisk cornstarch. 1 tablespoon water, soy sauce and sugar. Warm oil in a skillet over medium heat. Sauté coleslaw mix, water chestnuts, scallions and garlic until slaw has wilted, about 3 minutes. Stir in tofu; cook until hot and most of liquid has evaporated, about 3 minutes. Re-whisk cornstarch mixture and add to skillet. Cook, stirring, until thickened 1 to 2 minutes. Remove from heat. Lay one wrapper on a flat surface, along edge facing you. Spoon 1/4 cup tofu mixture on bottom third. Fold sides in toward center; roll tightly away from you, enclosing filling. Place seam side down on baking sheet. Repeat with remaining wrappers and filling. Moist tops of egg rolls with cooking spray. Bake until golden, 10-15 minutes. Serve immediately. Serves 8. I like Zhenjiang vinegar on the rolls or mustard.

Dad's Salsa Chili
LAVONNE STEVENSON

1 lb ground beef
1 medium onion, chopped
Dash of salt
15 oz can diced tomatoes with herb and garlic seasoning
15 oz can kidney beans, drained

Brown the ground beef. Add onion and cook till soft. Drain off excess grease. Add a dash of salt. Put all ingredients in crockpot. Cook for 7-8 hours. Serve.

Karon's Homemade Salsa (V)

KARON MICHEL, STRAY RESCUE FOSTER AND ADOPTIVE MOM

3 – 4 medium to large tomatoes, cored and cut into smaller pieces.
1 medium onion, diced
I bell pepper, diced
Either 1 can of diced green chilies or 1/2 jar of pickled jalapeño, depending on your spice preference*
Cilantro, chopped; to taste (optional)
1 tsp salt
½ tsp black pepper
2 Tbsp lime juice
1 Tbsp vinegar
½ tsp cumin (optional)

Add everything to your food processor and pulse until well chopped and blended. Best when refrigerated overnight

*If you use the jar of pickled jalapeño, omit the vinegar from the recipe as the juice contains vinegar.

Kathie's Deviled Eggs (V)

SUE WOODS

1 dozen eggs
¾ C Miracle Whip®
1 Tbsp mustard
Salt and Pepper

Boil eggs until hard (10 to 15 minutes.) Cool under cold running water for several minutes. Peel eggs, cut in half length-wise. Put yolks in a shallow bowl, put whites on an egg tray, plate or platter. Smash yolks with a fork; add salt and pepper to taste. In separate bowl, mix Miracle Whip with yellow mustard. Add this dressing to yolk and stir with fork until creamy. Taste to see if it needs more mustard. Put mixture into a baggie and cut off a small corner of baggie. Pipe mixture into the egg whites. Ready to serve or refrigerate until needed.

Beef & Onion Cheese Balls

MARCIA MATRECI

3 (8 oz) pkgs cream cheese, softened
2 (3 oz) pkgs Buddig Beef, diced
5 green onions, chopped (include tops)
1 tsp Accent®

Mix all ingredients together; mold into a ball. Serve with crackers.

Garlic Parmesan Roasted Chickpea Snack (V)
LINDA GRAMES

2 cans (15.5 oz each) garbanzo beans, rinsed and drained
2 Tbsp coconut oil, melted, divided
½ tsp salt
1 tsp garlic, minced, or more if you like
½ C grated Parmesan cheese
Dash cayenne powder or curry powder, to taste
Pepper, to taste

Drain the beans and rinse well. Lay them on paper towels to dry for about 30 minutes. Preheat oven to 400 degrees. In a bowl, mix together 1 tablespoon of oil and add chickpeas to coat. Add salt, garlic and cheese and stir well to coat. Lay beans on a baking sheet and drizzle with remaining tablespoon of melted coconut oil. Bake for 20 minutes, stir and continue to bake for up to an hour or until golden and crispy. Test batch was perfect at 45 minutes.

Cucumber Salsa (V)
DEB TEBRUGGE

2 C cucumber, finely chopped
½ C tomato, chopped
¼ C red onion, chopped
1 seeded jalapeño pepper, finely chopped
1 tsp garlic, minced
2 Tbsp fresh parsley
2 Tbsp fresh cilantro
¼ C plain Greek yogurt
1½ tsp lemon juice
1½ tsp lime juice
¼ tsp ground Cumin
¼ tsp seasoned salt

Combine first 7 ingredients. In another bowl, combine remaining ingredients. Pour over mixture and toss gently to coat. Serve with pita chips or tortilla chips. Great summer time dip.

Sweet Potato and Black Bean Chili (V)

CANDY WILEY, STRAY RESCUE FOSTER PARENT

3 sweet potatoes, peeled and diced
1 large red bell pepper, diced
1 medium white onion, diced
2 (14.5 oz) cans diced tomatoes, undrained (or 1 can diced tomatoes, undrained and 1 10 oz can Rotel with
   green chilies, undrained)
1 (14 oz) can tomato sauce (omit if you prefer thicker chili)
2 (15 oz) cans black beans, undrained
1 garlic clove, minced
1½ Tbsp chili powder
2 tsp cumin
1 tsp salt
½ tsp black pepper
Cheddar or other desired cheese/garnish

In a large slow cooker, combine all ingredients and mix well. Cover and cook on high for 4 hours or until potatoes are fork-tender. Garnish individual servings with cheese.

Cheddar Chowder (V)

MARY WHITEAKER

2 C potatoes, chopped
½ C celery, chopped
½ C carrots, chopped
¼ C onion, diced
2 C water
Salt and pepper to taste
¼ C butter
¼ C flour
2 C milk
2 C cheddar cheese, shredded
Optional ingredients: corn and ham

Bring water to boil. Add chopped vegetables and seasonings. Simmer until vegetables are done.
In a separate pan, melt butter, then add flour and mix well. Add milk and cheese, stirring until cheese melts. Add to the vegetable mixture and cook until hot, but not boiling.

Frogmore Stew

AMY COLE BUEHLER

6 qts water
4 lbs fresh shrimp, shells left on
2 lbs new red potatoes, scrubbed
2 lbs sausage (mixture of Andouille and smoked sausage is great) cut into chunks and sautéed until brown
12 ears corn, cut into 2 inch pieces
¾ C Old Bay® seasoning

Bring water and Old Bay to a boil in very large stockpot. Add potatoes and cook for 15 minutes. Add sausage and cook for 5 minutes more. Add corn and cook for another 5 minutes or so. Stir in the shrimp and cook until they turn pink (about 5 minutes.) Drain immediately and serve in a large bowl or spread on a table covered with newspaper. Serve with additional Old Bay, cocktail sauce, melted butter and crusty French bread. Serves 12.

West African Peanut Soup

PAT STRUCKEL, STRAY RESCUE VOLUNTEER

½ lb unsalted, shelled, roasted, ground peanuts
1 onion, finely chopped
4 C chicken stock
1 Tbsp cornstarch
1 C light cream
1 tsp salt
Freshly ground black pepper, to taste
⅛ tsp cayenne pepper
2 tsp paprika
1 Tbsp parsley or chives, finely chopped

Cook the peanuts and onion gently in the stock for 1 hour. Cool. Puree in blender. Stir cornstarch into cream and add to pureed soup. Season with salt and pepper. Add cayenne and paprika, and simmer for 10 minutes. Garnish with parsley or chives. Serves 4 to 6.

Autumn Chili

SHAWN BOEDEFELD, VOLUNTEER, DEDICATED TO NASH

1 large butternut squash, cooked and cubed
1½ lbs cooked chicken (or use a pre-cooked rotisserie chicken)
1 C green bell pepper, chopped
1 C onion, chopped
1 clove garlic, minced (or 1 Tbsp jarred, minced garlic)
1 tsp olive oil
1 (15 oz) can fire-roasted, garlic, diced tomatoes (Hunt's)
1 (15 oz) can white chili beans (Bush's)
1 (15.5 oz) can cannelloni beans (white kidney beans, Progresso)
1 C water
1 C apple cider (with cinnamon is good)
2 C chicken broth
¼ C packed brown sugar
1½ tsp chili powder
1½ tsp ground cumin
1½ tsp ground coriander
1½ tsp ground cinnamon
1½ tsp lemon garlic powder
1 tsp white pepper

Cut squash in half and remove seeds and pulp. Place cut-side down on a greased baking sheet. Bake at 350 degrees until tender (about 45 minutes.) Set aside to cool before removing skin and cubing. Sauté green pepper, onion and garlic heat until lightly browned and just tender. Put everything in a 5-quart crockpot and mix well. Cook on low for 2 – 3 hours, stirring occasionally. You can also add a can of sweet kernel corn or a can of hominy, if desired.

Taco Soup

LAVONNE STEVENSON

1½ lbs ground beef
1 large onion, chopped
1 envelope Hidden Valley Ranch® dressing mix
1 envelope taco seasoning mix
16 oz can pinto beans
16 oz can chili beans (regular or hot)
16 oz can whole kernel corn
16 oz can diced tomatoes

Brown the ground beef and onion together, drain. Mix in ranch dressing and taco seasoning mix into the meat. Without draining, add all the other ingredients into a crock pot and add the meat and stir. It's a thick soup, so if you want it thinner, add a little water. Cook on low for 6-8 hours. *Note: For a spicier soup, add 1 can of green chilies.*

Tailgating Chili

SARAH DENEAU, VOLUNTEER, ADOPTER, FOSTER

1 lb ground beef
1 lb ground pork
2 Tbsp olive oil
1 large onion, diced
1 green pepper, diced
1 jalapeño pepper, seeded and diced
3 cloves of garlic, minced
3 Tbsp green onion, diced
2 (15 oz) cans of chili beans, one hot, one mild
14.5 oz can diced tomatoes
6 oz tomato paste
8 oz tomato sauce
12 oz beer (your favorite)
2 Tbsp cornmeal
1 C water
¼ C chili powder (I usually do a little less)
1 Tbsp cumin
1 tsp garlic powder
½ tsp cayenne pepper
1 Tbsp salt
1½ tsp pepper
Dash of hot sauce to taste

Cook beef and pork in 6-quart Dutch oven until crumbly. Drain and discard grease. Remove from heat and set aside. In the same pot, heat olive oil. Sauté onion, green pepper, jalapeño and garlic. Add meat, green onion, beans, all tomatoes, beer and water. Season with chili powder, cumin, garlic powder, cayenne pepper, salt and pepper. Bring to simmer. Reduce to medium low. Cook 2 hours. Garnish with onion, cheese and sour cream. We like to serve it over Fritos. Makes 6 quarts.

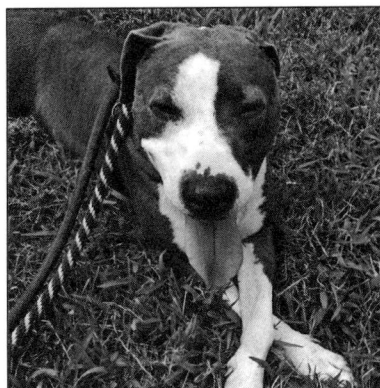

Stray Rescue – Edith

Lenny's Chili Blanco

LENORE HARNER FARIS

1 pound white (Navy) beans, rinsed
5-6 C chicken broth
1 tsp chicken stock base
2 white onions, chopped (use yellow if white are too strong)
1 Tbsp canola or vegetable oil
8-10 cloves garlic, minced
7 oz diced green chills
5 tsp ground cumin
2 tsp dried oregano leaves
½ tsp ground thyme
1-2 scant tsp cayenne pepper (less if you don't like it very hot)
5 C cooked and diced chicken
1 C sour cream
3 C shredded Monterey Jack cheese

To serve on top of chili:
Sour cream
Chopped green onions
Chopped cilantro
Diced tomatoes

Combine beans, broth and chicken stock base in a large pot. Simmer covered for 2 hours. Sauté onions in oil until golden. Add onions, garlic, green chilies, cumin, oregano, thyme, cayenne and chicken to bean mixture. Simmer another 30 minutes. Add sour cream and jack cheese. Heat until cheese melts. Serve with toppers listed above, warm flour tortillas or tortilla chips on the side. Cooking time is 2 hours 45 minutes. Freezes well if you do so before adding cheese and sour cream.

Uncle Donnie's Italian Bean Soup (V)

SHAWNA DAVINROY

2 celery stalks
2 large carrots
1 onion
1 zucchini
2 cans of white kidney beans (Cannelloni beans,) rinsed and drained
1 Tbsp olive oil
½ tsp dried basil or 1 tsp of fresh basil
1 can stewed tomatoes (Italian style)
1 can vegetable broth
2 C water
1 medium bunch of fresh spinach, cleaned well, chopped, stems removed (I always add more as spinach tends
  to cook down easily)
Parmesan cheese, grated
Fresh parsley, chopped
1 potato, chopped (for thickness, optional)
Salt and pepper, to taste

Clean and dice all vegetables. Mash beans until smooth. In a large Dutch oven, heat olive oil and add veggies, including spices and potato, over medium heat. Cook 12-15 minutes until veggies are tender. Stir in tomatoes, vegetable broth, spinach, water and mashed beans. Bring to a boil, reduce to low heat. Cover and simmer on low for about 20 minutes. Sprinkle with Parmesan cheese and serve. 🦴

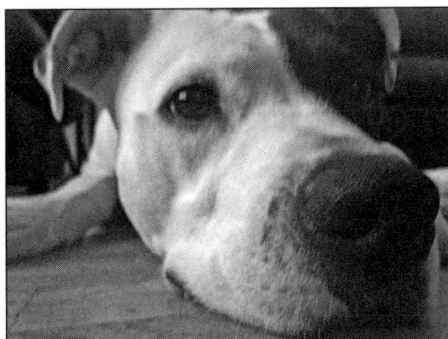

Stray Rescue – Aura

FRIENDS BEVERAGE

Red Sangria (V)

KRISTI JONES & DENNY LEWIS, HELPING HANDS FOR FURRY FRIENDS

1 orange
1 lemon
1 lime
¼ C sugar
1 750 ml bottle red wine (red Zinfandel works well, as does Shiraz or Syrah)
1 apple, sliced
1 peach sliced
¼ C orange juice
¼ C Triple Sec or Cointreau

Cut up and squeeze juice from the orange, lemon and lime into a large pitcher. Add smooshed rinds and sugar to pitcher, stirring well and pressing rinds against sides and bottom of pitcher. Add all remaining ingredients, stir well. Let sit 24 hours to blend flavors. Be sure to remove rinds after 24 hours. Stir again before serving.

Blue Sangria (V)

KRISTI JONES & DENNY LEWIS, HELPING HANDS FOR FURRY FRIENDS

1 (750 ml) bottle of Sauvignon Blanc wine
½ C blue Curacao
½ C fresh lemon juice
½ C Simple Syrup*
2 oranges, sliced
1 C pineapple chunks, preferably fresh

Mix everything together in a large pitcher. Let it sit 24 hours, then remove orange slices and enjoy.

*Simple Syrup: Bring 1 cup water and 1 cup sugar to a boil, stirring well. Turn down the heat and let simmer for 5 minutes. Remove from heat and cool completely before using.

Cranberry Margaritas (V)

KRISTI JONES & DENNY LEWIS, HELPING HANDS FOR FURRY FRIENDS

1 (12 oz.) can of limeade, thawed
1½ C tequila (fill up the empty limeade can with tequila)
½ C Triple Sec
4 C cranberry juice cocktail

Mix everything together in large pitcher and enjoy over ice.

Strawberry Daiquiri (V)

MELINDA SCHUSTER

1 shot rum
1½ shots sweet & sour mix or 1½ shots frozen lemonade
1 tsp powdered sugar
2 big shots frozen strawberries puree
Lots of ice

Mix in blender.

One summer when I was in my early 20s, my friend Audrey and I decided that we would find the best strawberry daiquiri in St. Louis. It was our goal for the summer. It took a great deal of diligence, but we found what we were looking for at the old Pavilion Restaurant in Dillard's at River Roads Shopping Center. The restaurant is gone now. In fact, River Roads Shopping Center is no longer in existence, but the recipe lives on.

Sparkling Bourbon Lemonade (V)

TRACEY HAMMACK

¾ C sugar
1 C fresh lemon juice
½ C fresh orange juice
1 qt cold club soda
1 lemon, sliced
1 orange, sliced
fresh mint sprigs, optional
4-6 shots bourbon (I like to use the honey bourbon)

Combine 1½ cups water and the sugar in a saucepan over high heat and cook until the sugar dissolves, about 2 minutes. Pour the syrup in a bowl, cover, and refrigerate until cold, at least 1 hour or up to one week. Combine syrup, lemon juice, and orange juice in a pitcher. Mix in club soda. Add lemon and orange slices and mint sprigs.Fill 4-6 glasses (depending on size) with crushed ice, add 1 shot bourbon to each and fill with the lemonade. Top with more mint if desired.

FRIENDS MAIN DISHES

Taco Pie

MARY WHITEAKER

1 deep-dish pie crust
1 onion, chopped
16 oz can refried beans
8 oz taco sauce or salsa
12 tortilla chips, crushed
1 lb ground beef
1 pkg taco seasoning
2 C cheddar cheese, shredded
Shredded lettuce
Chopped tomato

Heat oven and a cookie sheet to 400 degrees. Prick the sides and bottom of crust. Bake on heated cookie sheet for 10 minutes. Remove crust from oven and reduce heat to 350 degrees. Cook ground beef and onion until meat is brown; drain fat. Add taco seasoning and mix according to package directions. In a small bowl, mix refried beans and 1/3 cup of the taco sauce or salsa. Layer half of bean mixture in pie crust; top with half of meat mixture, then 1 cup of cheese and all of the crushed chips. Repeat the layers of beans, meat and cheese. Bake on heated cookie sheet 20-25 minutes. Top with remaining 2/3 cup taco sauce or salsa, lettuce and tomato.

Crockpot Tortellini (V)

KARON MICHEL, STRAY RESCUE FOSTER AND ADOPTIVE MOM

2 bags frozen tortellini
2 (32 oz)boxes vegetable broth
4 (14.5 oz) cans diced tomatoes with garlic and onion
2 (8 oz) blocks cream cheese
½ bag fresh spinach
2 tsp fresh garlic
Parmesan cheese for garnish (optional)

Place all ingredients except Parmesan cheese in the crockpot. Cook on low for 5-6 hours.

Sausage Rigatoni

KAREN S. FREEBERSYSER

½ (1 lb) hot Italian sausage*
½ (1 lb) sweet Italian sausage*
1 green pepper, chopped
1 red pepper, chopped
1 onion, chopped
1 zucchini, chopped
1 C mushrooms, chopped
16 oz pasta, rigatoni or Penne Rigate
1 (14.5 oz) can stewed tomatoes
1 (8 oz) can tomato sauce
2 Tbsp olive oil
2 Tbsp basil
2 Tbsp oregano
3 gloves garlic
1 tsp red pepper
Parmesan cheese

In a large skillet, cook sausage; remove from heat and set aside. Discard most of the grease. In same skillet, heat olive oil and add all chopped vegetables and seasonings. Cook until soft. Add stewed tomatoes, tomato sauce and cooked sausage. Cover and cook on medium to low for 30 minutes. Pour over pasta and top with grated Parmesan cheese. **I remove casing and make small sausage balls.*

Parmesan Cheese Sauce (V)

BARB LUNDEEN

4½ pints heavy whipping cream
20 oz Parmesan cheese, grated
1 stick butter

In a double boiler, melt butter. Add Parmesan cheese and whipping cream until smooth. Bring just to a boil and reduce heat. Let simmer for 3-4 minutes until thickened. Makes approximately 8 cups. I usually cut this recipe in half. If you want, add minced garlic. Serve with your favorite cooked pasta.

Slow Cooker Mushroom Spinach Lasagna (V)

KARON MICHEL, STRAY RESCUE FOSTER AND ADOPTIVE MOM

Non-stick cooking spray
1 Tbsp olive oil
1 (8 oz) pkg fresh mushrooms, sliced
1 (6 oz)pkg baby spinach leaves
1 (14.5 oz) can diced tomatoes with garlic and onion
2 C tomato sauce
½ tsp dried Italian seasoning
¼ tsp salt
8 oz cottage cheese, drained
½ C Parmesan cheese, grated and divided
¼ tsp ground black pepper
6 dry lasagna noodles, uncooked
1½ C shredded Italian blend cheese, divided

Spray inside of 4-quart slow cooker with cooking spray. Combine cottage cheese, 1/4 cup Parmesan cheese and pepper in small bowl; set aside. Make sauce: heat oil in large skillet over medium-high heat. Add mushrooms; cook 3 minutes, stirring occasionally. Add spinach; cook 3 minutes more or until mushrooms are tender and spinach is wilted, stirring occasionally. Stir in undrained tomatoes, tomato sauce, Italian seasoning and salt. Bring to a boil. Reduce heat and simmer 3 minutes, stirring occasionally. Spread 3/4 cup sauce mixture over bottom of slow cooker. Layer 3 lasagna noodles over sauce mixture, breaking noodles to fit. Top with 3/4 cup sauce mixture, cottage cheese mixture and 1 cup Italian cheese. Top with 3/4 cup sauce mixture and remaining 3 lasagna noodles, breaking to fit. Spoon remaining sauce mixture over noodles. Cover; cook on low for 5 hours or until noodles are tender. Sprinkle with remaining 1/2 cup Italian cheese and remaining 1/4 cup Parmesan cheese. Cover; let stand 5 minutes or until cheese melts.

Beer Barbecue Beef Brisket

AMY COLE BUEHLER

½ C Weber Kansas City-style Barbecue Rub®
¼ C brown sugar
1 (4-5 lb.) beef brisket, fat cap trimmed and scored
1 C beef broth
1 16 oz beer

Preheat oven to 350 degrees. Mix together the rub and brown sugar. Rub onto both sides of brisket. Place in a foil-lined roasting pan and bake uncovered for 1 hour. Decrease oven temp to 300 degrees and pour the beef broth and beer around the brisket. Cover tightly with foil and bake for 3 hours. Let rest 30 minutes before slicing.

Spinach Soufflé Quiche

ARLENE RIORDAN

1 unbaked 9" pie shell
1 medium onion, chopped
6 slices bacon, chopped
8 eggs
½ C sour cream
½ C light cream
¼ tsp salt
⅛ tsp white pepper (black pepper will do)
Dash ground nutmeg
3 C fresh spinach, lightly packed
⅔ C mozzarella cheese, shredded
½ C Swiss cheese, shredded

Preheat oven to 300 degrees. Cook onion and bacon in skillet. Drain on paper towels. In a medium bowl, beat eggs slightly. Stir in sour cream, cream, salt, pepper and nutmeg. Stir in onion mixture, spinach and cheeses. Pour into pastry shell. Bake 45-50 minutes or until knife inserted near center comes out clean. Let stand 10 minutes before serving. 🦴

Flank Steak Marinade

MARYANNE GALLAGHER-BURNS

½ C water
⅓ C lemon juice
½ C ketchup
2 Tbsp Worcestershire sauce
8 drops Tabasco
3 bay leaves
½ tsp basil
½ tsp celery seed
½ tsp cracked black pepper

Combine all ingredients in medium saucepan; bring to boil and simmer 7-10 minutes. Lay flank steak out in 9" x 13" Pyrex dish. Score steak and pour small amount of the marinade under the steak, then the remaining on the side scored (scored side up.) For best results, let stand for 30 minutes, then refrigerate 3-4 hours. Barbecue on medium-high heat for 10-12 minutes on each side for medium rare. Best if recipe is doubled. 🦴

Amy's Spaghetti Sauce

AMY COLE BUEHLER

2 lbs Italian sausage
1 large onion, chopped
1 green pepper, chopped
1 red, yellow or orange pepper, chopped
4 cloves garlic, chopped
½ C. dry red wine
2 Tbsp Italian seasoning
1 (28 oz) can Cento brand San Marzano® crushed tomatoes
1 (15 oz) can Cento brand San Marzano® petite diced tomatoes
2 Tbsp ketchup
1 tsp Worcestershire sauce
Salt and pepper
1 (8 oz) pkg mushrooms, pre-sliced
1 Tbsp butter

Cook sausage in a large Dutch oven for about 10-15 minutes on medium until brown and crumbled. Add onions peppers and garlic. Cook for an additional 7-8 minutes on medium-low until meat is cooked through and vegetables are soft and starting to caramelize. Drain the sausage mixture and put back into the pot. Add the red wine and Italian seasoning; mix well and let cook for about 2 minutes, stirring constantly until liquid is almost evaporated. Add the tomatoes, ketchup, Worcestershire sauce, and salt and pepper to taste. Simmer over very low heat, uncovered (or partially covered) for 1 1/2-2 hours, stirring occasionally. Brown the mushrooms in the butter in a non-stick skillet until nicely colored and their liquid is evaporated. Add to sauce and stir. Serve with any shape pasta and Parmesan cheese on the side. The key to this sauce is to simmer it over low heat for a few hours. This concentrates the flavors and tightens the sauce so that it won't be watery and run on the plate. 🦴

Minnesota Tater Tot Hot Dish Casserole

SHERRY DENEAU, MOM TO STRAY RESCUE ALUM, MILLIE (FORMERLY RAVIOLI)

1 lb ground beef
1 medium onion, chopped
1 (10¾ oz) cream of mushroom soup
1 (10¾ oz)cream of chicken soup
½ C milk
16 oz pkg frozen mixed vegetables
16 oz pkg frozen Tater Tots
1½ C Cheddar Jack cheese

Brown ground beef with onion; drain off fat. Stir in soups, milk and vegetables. Transfer mixture to a 9" x 13" baking dish. Arrange Tater Tots on top. Bake in 350 degree pre-heated oven for about 30 minutes or until mixture is bubbly and Tater Tots are brown and crisp. Sprinkle cheese over Tater Tots and return dish to oven. Bake for 10-15 minutes or until cheese melts. Serves 8. 🦴

Filipino Chicken and Pork Adobo

ARLENE RIORDAN

4 pieces of chicken and 2 pork steaks cut into 3 pieces (or you can use all chicken, 6-8 pieces)
1 C soy sauce
1 C white vinegar
2 C water
1 tsp garlic powder
1 tsp MSG
1 tsp whole black or mixed colored peppercorns, place in a metal tea leaf container (if you don't have one, then omit peppercorns and use a dash ground pepper
2 bay leaves
2-3 cloves fresh garlic, smashed or diced
1 small onion, chopped
2 additional cloves garlic, smashed or diced
1 (14.5 oz) can diced tomatoes (or 1 medium/large tomato, chopped)

If using pork, mix ingredients and add pork and bring to a boil. Cover and simmer on low for 45 minutes-1 hour. Add chicken, bring to a boil then turn down to low, cover and simmer for another half hour. If using only chicken, bring to a boil, cover then simmer for 30 minutes. Add onions, additional garlic and diced tomatoes and bring to a boil for a couple minutes, stirring frequently. Turn down heat, cover and simmer an additional 10-15 minutes. Serve over hot white rice. 🦴

Hot Chicken Salad

SHERRY DENEAU, MOM TO STRAY RESCUE ALUM, MILLIE (FORMERLY RAVIOLI)

2 C chicken, cooked and cubed
2 Tbsp lemon juice
2 C cooked rice
¾ C mayonnaise
1 (10¾ oz) can cream of chicken soup
1 (10¾oz) can cream of mushroom soup
1 C celery, chopped
½ C water chestnuts
½ C pimentos
½ C sliced almonds
2 Tbsp chopped onion
1 C cheddar cheese, shredded
1 C potato chips, crushed

Cool chicken; cube and marinate in lemon juice for 1 hour. Mix the remaining ingredients (except for the cheese and chips.) Add chicken. Pour mixture into 9" x 13" greased pan. Top with cheese and chips. Bake at 350 degree oven for 30-40 minutes or until bubbly. 🦴

Oran's Rice Casserole

MARIANNE JUNGER, STAFF AT STRAY RESCUE

1 lb R.B. Rice's Pork Sausage, medium or hot
1 (8 oz) box River Rice
1 onion, chopped
½ C celery, chopped
2 (10.5 oz) cans cream of mushroom soup (or cream of celery soup)
2 (10.5 oz) cans cream of chicken soup
1½ soup cans of water
Shredded or sliced cheddar cheese for topping
8 oz pkg slivered almonds, optional

Brown pork sausage in skillet. Mix sausage, rice, onion, celery, both soups and water in a 9" x 13" pan. Cover and bake at 350 degrees for 1 hour. Top with cheddar cheese and almonds after 45 minutes of baking and return to oven uncovered for additional 15 minutes or until cheese starts to melt.

Honey Bourbon BBQ Sauce (V)

KRISTI JONES & DENNY LEWIS, HELPING HANDS FOR FURRY FRIENDS

2 Tbsp olive oil
½ yellow onion, diced
2 C ketchup
1 C apple cider vinegar
1 C molasses
½ C honey
1 Tbsp Dijon® style or spicy brown mustard
¾ tsp chili powder
¾ tsp ground black pepper
¼ C whiskey (Jack Daniels preferred)

Cook onion in olive oil over medium heat just until soft. Add remaining ingredients except whiskey. Simmer over low heat 30-40 minutes, stirring occasionally. Add more chili powder and black pepper for a spicier sauce. Remove from heat; add whiskey. Serve with meat of your choice.

RECIPES TO THE RESCUE 2

Summertime Marinade for Steak, Chicken or Anything Else You Can Think Of (V)

KRISTI JONES & DENNY LEWIS, HELPING HANDS FOR FURRY FRIENDS

¼ C whiskey (Jack Daniels® preferred)
¼ C soy sauce
¼ C Dijon® style or spicy brown mustard
¼ C chopped green onion
¼ C brown sugar
1 tsp salt
Dash Worcestershire® sauce
Dash ground black pepper

Mix all the ingredients together, stirring until brown sugar is dissolved.

Vegan Mock Chicken Salad (V)

SHAWNA DAVINROY

12 oz tempeh, cubed
2 stalks of celery, minced
1 red bell pepper, minced
1 large dill pickle, minced
2-3 scallions, minced
1 Tbsp fresh parsley, chopped
½ C vegan mayonnaise (I prefer Veganaise® brand made with grapeseed oil)
1 Tbsp yellow mustard
1 tsp lemon juice
Salt and pepper to taste

Boil cubed tempeh in salted water for about 12-15 minutes and set aside to cool (I usually just toss it in the fridge.) In a large bowl, combine celery, pepper, pickle, scallion and parsley. Run a knife through the tempeh to give it a rough chop and add to bowl, along with the mayonnaise, mustard, lemon and salt and pepper. Fold everything together, cover and refrigerate for at least 30 minutes to let the flavors marry. Will keep in the refrigerator for up to five days.

Sweet Potato and Black Bean Enchiladas (V)

SHAWNA DAVINROY

Green Chili Sauce
1 C vegetable broth
1 Tbsp corn starch, dissolved in a little cold water
1 C roasted green chiles, chopped, hot or mild (be generous)
2-3 cloves garlic, minced
1 tsp cumin or chili powder, to taste

Enchilada Filling
1 (15 oz) can black beans, rinsed and drained
4 cloves garlic, minced
Fresh lime juice from 1 lime
2 heaping C of cooked and diced sweet potatoes (microwave for 5-6 minutes, then dice)
½ C roasted mild green chilies, chopped
½ tsp ground cumin
½ tsp chili powder, mild or spicy
2 Tbsp chopped fresh cilantro
Salt and pepper, to taste
8 white or yellow corn tortillas
4 oz Monterey jack cheese, shredded

Preheat oven to 350 degrees. Baking dish must hold 8 enchiladas. Make the green chile sauce by combining the broth, dissolved cornstarch, green chiles, garlic and spices in a saucepan and cook over medium-high heat until thickened. Set aside. For the enchilada filling, combine the drained black beans with minced garlic and lime juice. Toss to coat the beans and set aside. In a separate bowl, combine the cooked sweet potatoes with the chopped green chilies; add the spices. Season with salt and pepper. Pour about 1/4 cup of the green chile sauce into the bottom of the baking dish. Lay the first tortilla in the sauced baking dish. Wet it with the sauce. Spoon 1/8 of the sweet potato mixture down the center. Top with 1/8 of the black bean mixture. Wrap and roll the tortilla and place at the end of the baking dish. Repeat for the remaining tortillas. Top with the rest of sauce and sprinkle the shredded Monterey Jack cheese on top. Bake for 20-25 minutes until the enchiladas are hot and the sauce is bubbling around the edges.

Note: Can substitute 1 jar of verde salsa for the green chile sauce.

Apricot/Mustard Chicken Breasts

TINA MICELI, ADOPTER, VOLUNTEER AND ENRICHMENT TEAM MEMBER

4-6 bone-in, skin-on chicken breasts
½ C Grey Poupon® mustard
¼ C Smucker's® apricot preserves
Salt, pepper (or seasoned salt,) garlic powder, to taste

Preheat oven to 350 degrees. Rinse chicken breasts in cold water, pat dry. Massage chicken for few minutes to insure tenderness. Arrange chicken in pan. Pour over chicken mixture of 2-to-1 mustard to preserves. Bake at 350 degrees about one hour. Check thickest part of chicken for doneness (no longer pink.) Skin will brown nicely. 🦴

Reuben Casserole

LAVONNE STEVENSON FOREST LAKE, MN

20 oz bag shredded frozen hash browns
¼ tsp salt
¼ tsp pepper
1½ lbs lean corn beef, sliced
¼ C Russian dressing
16 oz ounce can sauerkraut, drained well
8 slices Swiss cheese

Heat oven to 450 degrees. Put the shredded frozen hash browns in a greased 13" x 9" x 2" baking dish. Season with ¼ teaspoon of each salt and pepper. Bake at 450 degrees for 15 minutes. Top with the corn beef, slightly overlapping. Spread the Russian dressing on top. Spoon the well-drained, sauerkraut over the top. Cover with 8 slices of Swiss cheese. Bake at 450 degrees for 15 more minutes. Serve with extra dressing on the side. Serves 8. 🦴

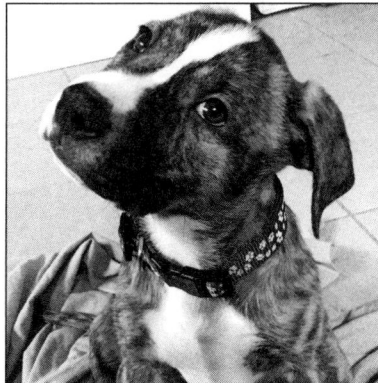

Stray Rescue – Elliott

Chicken Enchiladas

RHONDA SHULTS

4 chicken breasts or whole chicken, cooked and shredded
2 (10.5 oz) cans cream of mushroom soup
1 (10.5 oz) can cream of chicken soup
1 tsp cumin
8 oz sour cream
4-5 green onions, chopped
1 pkg medium flour tortillas
8 oz bag Colby Jack shredded cheese or Mexican mix, non-seasoned
Small jar salsa (your favorite kind)
Small can enchilada sauce (red sauce, not green)

Preheat oven to 350 degrees. Spray 11" x 13" glass or metal pan with cooking spray. Spread thin layer of salsa on entire bottom of pan. Mix first 6 ingredients along with half bag of the shredded cheese and mix well. Fill approx. 6-7 flour tortillas with mix, roll and place open end down in pan. Leave enough mix leftover to spread over top of enchiladas once the pan is full. Sprinkle remaining cheese over the top and pour entire can of enchilada sauce over the cheese. Bake at 350 degrees for 30-45 minutes or until semi-browned.

Chicken Pot Pie

NANCY SCHULZE

1 pkg refrigerated pie dough (one that has two crusts)
1 (10.5 oz) can cream of chicken soup
1 (10.5 oz)can cream of potato or mushroom or celery (depends on your preference)
1 tsp poultry seasoning
½ C onion, chopped
2 C cooked and diced chicken (can use a rotisserie chicken and shred the meat)
1 bag frozen mixed vegetables (don't defrost)
Salt and Pepper, to taste

In a deep-dish pie plate or small casserole dish, place the crust on bottom. In a large mixing bowl, add all remaining ingredients and mix. Pour the mixture onto of the bottom crust. Then place top crust and make vent holes in the crust for baking. Bakes at 350 degrees for about 1 hour and 15 minutes or until crust is golden brown and inside is hot.

Lomo Saltado

RICK MENDOZA

12 oz ribeye steak or similar
16 oz pkg frozen french fries
Vegetable oil, as needed
Salt, pepper and garlic, to taste
1 large onion, sliced into strips
3 large tomatoes, peeled, seeded and sliced into strips
1 yellow chile pepper (preferably Peruvian aji Amarillo)
¼ C distilled white vinegar
1 dash soy sauce, to taste
2-3 pinches chopped parsley leaves
Steamed white rice for serving

Cut the steak in long pieces, ¼ inch by 2 inches. Season with salt, pepper and garlic to taste. Prepare the bag of French fries according to package directions. Heat the oil in a frying pan over medium-high heat. Fry the meat until just cooked and juices begin to release. Remove the meat from the frying pan and cook the onions until they are transparent. Stir in the tomato and pepper. Cook until the tomato softens. Pour in the vinegar and soy sauce. Add the meat with its juice, the French fries; cover and cook until the beef is done, about 3 minutes. Season to taste with salt and pepper, and sprinkle with chopped parsley. Serve with rice.

Chicken Tetrazzini

RHONDA SHULTS

16 oz thin spaghetti, cooked (or any of your favorite noodles)
½ C butter (plus more for buttering pan)
4 chicken breasts, cooked, diced
2 (10.5 oz) cans cream of chicken soup
2 C sour cream
1 tsp kosher salt
½ tsp ground black pepper
2 Tbsp Parmesan cheese
2 C mozzarella cheese, shredded

Preheat oven to 300 degrees. Combine butter, cooked chicken, soup, sour cream, salt and pepper. Add cooked noodles. Pour into a buttered 13" x 9" baking pan. Sprinkle both cheeses on top and cover with foil. Bake for 45 minutes. Remove foil and bake for another 15 minutes. May be made in advance and refrigerated before cooking, however, add time to heat thoroughly.

Bastilla

TODD ELLER, VOLUNTEER

2 chickens, cut into pieces; skin breasts, thighs and legs
Poaching liquid
½ C white wine
2 Tbsp salt
1 Tbsp pepper
2 stalks celery
2 carrots
1 onion
1 bay leaf
Water to cover

In a large stock pot or Dutch oven, add the poaching liquid ingredients, then the chicken pieces. Add enough water to cover the chicken. Poach the dark meat first and then add the white. Remove the chicken and strain the poaching liquid and reserve. Shred the chicken.

Filling:
1 onion, finely chopped
¼ C fresh parsley, minced; mince first, then measure
2 Tbsp cilantro, minced
¼ tsp ground turmeric
8 threads saffron, toasted and crushed
1 C water
1 tsp ground ginger
1¼ tsp ground cinnamon
3 eggs, slightly beaten (think scrambled eggs)
Salt & pepper
⅔ C powdered sugar +

Almond mixture
½ C whole blanched almonds
½ C powdered sugar
1 tsp ground cinnamon
12 sheets phyllo dough, thawed
1 C butter, melted; measure, then melt
Garnish with cinnamon and powdered sugar

Preheat oven to 425 degrees. In heavy saucepan, sauté onion 8-10 minutes until golden, but not brown. Add parsley, cilantro, turmeric, saffron, water, ginger and cinnamon. Simmer about 20 min. Add eggs and scramble; season with salt, pepper and powdered sugar. Stir in shredded blanched chicken. Layer in this order: buttered phyllo, buttered phyllo, buttered phyllo, almond mixture; buttered phyllo, buttered phyllo, buttered phyllo, chicken mixture (centered); buttered phyllo, buttered phyllo, buttered phyllo, almond mixture; buttered phyllo, buttered phyllo, buttered phyllo. Tuck the top under the bottom and place on a baking sheet (pizza pan works great.) Bake 20-25 min at 425 degrees. Garnish with cinnamon and powdered sugar. 🦴

5 Cheese Macaroni and Cheese (V)

SARAH DENEAU, VOLUNTEER, ADOPTER, FOSTER PARENT

1 Tbsp vegetable oil
1 lb macaroni
1 stick butter, plus 1 Tbsp butter
4 oz Muenster cheese, cut into pieces
8 oz bag shredded Monterey Jack, Mild Cheddar and Sharp Cheddar Mixture (or 1/2 C of each)
8 oz Velveeta Shreds®
4 oz cream cheese, room temperature
2 C half and half
2 eggs, beaten
¼ tsp seasoned salt
⅛ tsp pepper
3 Tbsp brown sugar
½ tsp hot sauce
1 tsp yellow mustard

Preheat oven to 350 degrees. Mix all the shredded cheeses together in a bowl. Add oil to pot of salted boiling water. Add macaroni and cook till tender. Drain well. Return to pot and add 1 stick of butter, Half and Half, eggs, cream cheese, brown sugar, mustard, hot sauce and half of the cheese mixture. Season with salt and pepper. Transfer to 2½ quart casserole. Top with remaining cheese and dot with 1 tablespoon butter. Bake about 35 minutes until bubbly around the edges.

Tina's Favorite Lemon-Butter Chicken

TINA MICELI, ADOPTER, VOLUNTEER AND ENRICHMENT TEAM MEMBER

One chicken, cut up
6-8 fresh lemons, squeezed
½ stick butter, cut in slices for each chicken piece
Seasoned salt, to taste
Garlic powder, to taste
Pepper, to taste

Wash and pat dry chicken pieces. Place chicken in pan, skin-side up. Season well. Top each piece of chicken with a slice of butter. Broil until chicken skin starts to brown, then turn and broil other side. About half way through cooking, add lemon juice to the meat. Continue broiling carefully until meat is done. Serve with a salad and crusty bread.

Easy, Yummy Oven Baked Ribs

CHERYL LINNEMAN

1 *slab ribs*
1 *C brown sugar*
1 *small bottle of your favorite barbecue sauce*

In a 13" x 9" oven-safe, disposable pan, place ribs, then pack the brown sugar on top. Add barbecue sauce. Bake uncovered at 250 degrees for 7-8 hours. Cover with foil the last couple of hours as the barbecue sauce will thicken up around the ribs.

Honey Pecan Chicken Salad

JO OBERG FROM GRANDMA KAREN LARSON

3 *C medium shell macaroni*
3 *C cooked chicken breast, cut in large pieces*
2 *C red seedless grapes, halved*
4 *C chopped romaine lettuce*
2 *C broccoli*
½ *C red onion strips*
Broken pecan pieces, toasted
Dressing, whisk ingredients together:
¾ *C mayo*
¾ *C sour cream*
1 *Tbsp honey*
1 *Tbsp dijon mustard*
1 *tsp salt*
½ *tsp pepper*

Cook pasta. Drain and rinse with cold water. In large bowl, combine pasta, chicken, grapes, lettuce, broccoli and onion. One hour before serving, pour dressing over salad and toss. Adjust seasonings as needed. Cover and refrigerate. Add pecans just before serving.

Quick and Easy Turkey Pot Pie

TODD BOHNSACK, FROM AN OLD FAMILY COOKBOOK

10 ounce package refrigerated biscuits
3 cups cooked cubed turkey
1½ C cooked frozen peas and carrots
½ C chopped celery
⅓ C chopped onion
1 tsp seasoned salt
½ tsp salt
⅓ tsp rosemary leaves
⅛ tsp white pepper
⅛ tsp poultry seasoning
1¼ C cream of mushroom soup
⅔ cup undiluted evaporated milk
2 Tbsp lemon juice.

Roll out each biscuit to about 3½ half inch in diameter and press around sides and bottom of buttered 10 by 6 by 2 inch baking dish. Prick with fork and bake in oven at 375 degrees for 5 minutes or until partially baked. Combine remaining ingredients in large mixing bowl and mix well. Spoon turkey mixture into partially baked crust. Return to oven and bake an additional 25 minutes.

Lemon Chicken

KAREN S. FREEBERSYSER

3 or 4 small cans golden mushroom soup
2 tsp paprika
½ tsp salt
½ tsp lemon pepper
¾ tsp tarragon, crushed between fingers
6 Tbsp lemon juice (less for less tangy and tart sauce)
2 lbs chicken pieces (fillets or nugget-size pieces)
Lemon slices

Preheat the oven to 350 degrees. In a large bowl, combine the soup, paprika, salt, lemon pepper, tarragon, and lemon juice. Spread a small amount of the mixture on the bottom of a casserole dish to prevent the chicken from sticking. Arrange the chicken pieces in the casserole. Pour the remaining mixture over the chicken. Cover with a lid or foil. Bake for 1 hour. Before serving, cut the lemon into 1/4 inch slices; make a cut halfway through lemon circle. Twist in opposite directions at the slit (180 degrees). Garnish. Tip: Can be made in a crock-pot. Cook for 4 to 6 hours on high or for 8 to 10 hours on low. Serve over rice.

Sloppy Joe's

KAREN S. FREEBERSYSER

1 (14.5 oz) can whole tomatoes
1 (8 oz) can tomato paste
1 (8 oz) can tomato sauce
⅓ package of Chili-O-Mix®
2 lbs ground beef
1 small onion, chopped
2 Tbsp sugar
½ tsp pepper
½ tsp salt

Brown ground beef and onions separately, then drain. Add onions, whole tomatoes, tomato sauce, and tomato paste to hamburger. Break up the whole tomatoes while in skillet. Add one small can of water. Let come to a boil. When comes to a boil, add Chili-O-Mix. Add sugar, pepper, and salt last. Let simmer 30 minutes. Spoon onto a bun. Serve with a pickle wedge.

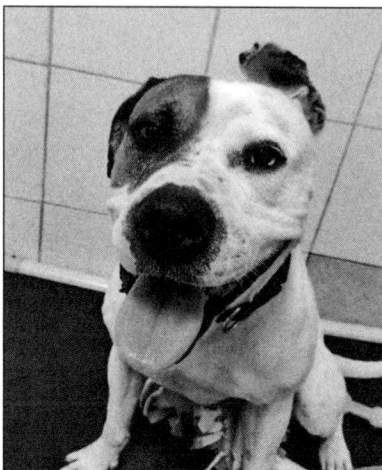

Stray Rescue – Knuckles

FRIENDS SIDE DISHES

Zucchini, Squash and Corn Casserole (V)

MELISSA OBERNUEFEMANN, STRAY RESCUE VOLUNTEER

1½ lbs yellow squash, cut into ¼ inch thick slices
1½ lbs zucchini, cut into 1/4 inch thick slices
¼ C butter, divided
2 C diced sweet onion
2 garlic cloves, minced
3 C fresh corn kernels
6 oz white cheddar cheese, freshly shredded
½ C sour cream
½ C mayonnaise
2 large eggs, lightly beaten
2 tsp black pepper
1 tsp table salt
1½ C soft, fresh breadcrumbs, divided
1 C Asiago cheese, freshly grated, divided

Preheat oven 350 degrees. Bring zucchini, yellow squash and water to a boil over medium-high heat and boil 5 minutes or until crisp-tender. Drain and gently press between paper towels. Cut fresh corn off the cob and set aside. Melt 2 tablespoons butter in skillet over medium heat; add onion and sauté 10 minutes or until tender. Add garlic and sauté 2 minutes. Stir together squash/zucchini, onion mixture, corn, white cheddar, sour cream, mayo, eggs, pepper and salt. Mix in ½ cup of bread crumbs and ½ cup Asiago cheese until blended. Spoon mixture into lightly greased 13" x 9" baking dish. Melt remaining 2 tablespoons butter. Stir in remaining 1 cup breadcrumbs and remaining ½ cup Asiago cheese. Sprinkle over casserole. Bake at 350 degrees for 45-50 minutes or until golden brown. Let stand for 10 minutes before serving.

*I use store bought, canned breadcrumbs and shredded Asiago cheese and it all works the same. Also, sometimes I add a few florets of cauliflower to the recipe. 🦴

Central Market Cranberry Relish (V)

DEBRA MCSTAY

1 (12 oz) pkg fresh cranberries
1 apple, chopped
1 Clementine orange, sections halved
2 Tbsp fresh ginger
1½ C fresh squeezed orange juice
2 C sugar
1 tsp cracked black pepper

Combine all ingredients in a heavy bottom saucepan over medium-high heat. Cook until cranberries burst (15-20 minutes.) Chill to serve.

Crunchy Asian Coleslaw

BECKY SLATIN

16 oz bag of coleslaw
1 bunch green onions, chopped
Crunchy Mix:
2 pkgs Ramen® Chicken Noodles (set Ramen® seasoning packets aside for dressing; I put the Ramen noodles in a Ziploc bag and crush with a jar)
½ C slivered almonds
4 Tbsp sesame seeds
3 Tbsp butter

Dressing:
⅔ C oil
2 Tbsp rice vinegar
2 Tbsp soy sauce
4 Tbsp sugar
1 tsp pepper
Ramen seasoning packets

Melt butter and brown Ramen noodles, almonds and sesame seeds; let cool and store in Ziploc bag or airtight container for tossing. I usually make this the night before to save time. Mix and toss dressing with slaw, onions and dry mix before serving.

Pasta Salad (V)

ARLENE RIORDAN

1 lb noodles (spiral, macaroni, your choice)
½ C oil
1½ C sugar
1⅓ C vinegar
2 tsp mustard
2 tsp garlic powder
2 tsp celery seed
2 tsp chopped parsley flakes
2 tsp salt
2 tsp pepper
1 C pimentos, chopped
1 C white onion, chopped (I use sweet onions)
1 C cucumber, chopped and peeled

Mix together sugar, vinegar, mustard, garlic powder, celery seed, chopped parsley flakes, salt, pepper, pimentos, white onion, cucumber in a very large bowl or pot and set aside. Cook noodles as directed, drain, and while hot, toss with 1/2 cup oil. While still hot, pour marinade dressing on noodles. Marinate at least 24 hours.

You can also add: (not all items are vegetarian)
1 lb sharp cheddar cheese, cubed (while pasta is cold!)
¼ lb hard salami, cut into small squares
1 (2.5 oz) can sliced black olives
1 (14 oz) can artichokes, cut into small pieces
1 pepper, chopped (whatever color you like)
Fresh broccoli
Zucchini

Corn in a Crockpot (V)

ARLENE RIORDAN

3 (16 oz) pkgs frozen corn
1 stick butter, cut into pieces
1 (8 oz) pkg cream cheese, cut into chunks
¼ C sugar

Place all ingredients in a crock pot and cook for 4 hours on high. Stir every hour.

Pasta Salad Capresi (V)

AMY COLE BUEHLER

16 oz bow tie or other short pasta
1 small carton sweet grape tomatoes, halved with a few left whole
1 large ball or braid of fresh Mozzarella, cut into small chunks
Several handfuls of fresh basil, cut into a chiffonade (long strips)
Shredded Parmesan cheese, to taste
Salt and pepper, to taste
Salad dressing: I prefer a mix of creamy Caesar with Vivienne's Romano Cheese® dressing. Anything you like will work though.

Cook pasta according to package directions, drain, rinse and chill. Toss chilled pasta with remaining ingredients. Add salt and pepper to taste. Chill a bit longer until serving. Check seasonings before serving -- the pasta has a tendency to soak up the dressing and you may want to add more.

Variation: add cold, cooked chicken or shrimp.

Roasted Brussels Sprouts with Lemon (V)

SHAWNA DAVINROY

2½ lbs Brussels sprouts, trimmed and halved
2 cloves garlic, smashed
3 Tbsp olive oil
6 Tbsp unsalted butter, melted
⅓ C bread crumbs
3 Tbsp fresh lemon juice
1 tsp salt (or to taste)
½ tsp pepper (or to taste)

Heat oven to 425 degrees. In a large bowl, toss the Brussels sprouts, garlic, olive oil, salt and pepper. Divide evenly on 2 rimmed baking sheets and roast, tossing halfway through, until tender (15-20 minutes.) Transfer Brussels sprouts to a large bowl. Add the butter, bread crumbs and lemon juice and toss to combine.

*Brussels sprouts can be roasted up to 1 day in advance; refrigerate and cover. Reheat in the microwave, covered with a damp paper towel. This is one of those recipes that has been known to change a sprout hater's mind.

Creamy Potato Salad (V)

KAREN S. FREEBERSYSER

10 medium potatoes
1 C celery, chopped
½ C onion, finely chopped
⅓ C sweet pickles, chopped
1¼ C mayonnaise (Hellmann's®)
3 tsp sugar
2½ tsp vinegar
2 tsp yellow mustard
2-3 tsp salt
5 hard-boiled eggs, coarsely chopped
Paprika

In a covered saucepan, cook the potatoes in boiling salted water for 25 to 30 minutes or until tender; drain well and transfer to a large bowl. Peel and cube the potatoes. Add celery, onion and sweet pickles. In a separate bowl, combine mayonnaise, sugar, vinegar, mustard and salt. Add the mayonnaise mixture to the potatoes and toss lightly to coat. Carefully fold in the chopped eggs. Sprinkle with paprika. Cover and chill thoroughly before serving. (Hint: if mixture seems dry, add a little more mayonnaise.)

Spaghetti Squash Casserole (V)

MICHELLE STREIFF, VOLUNTEER, FOSTER, ADOPTER

1 Spaghetti squash
1 lg onion
¼ C butter, unsalted
½ C water
½ C sour cream
Kosher salt and pepper to taste
2 C Monterey Jack Cheese, grated
Paprika

Microwave whole squash for 1 minute to soften. Cut squash in half lengthwise and remove seeds. Place cut side down on sheet pan, add 1/2 cup water, roast in oven till soft, about 30-45 minutes, or microwave in casserole for 12 minutes. When cooled slightly, remove squash from shell and set aside. Meanwhile, sauté chopped onion in butter until just beginning to brown. Remove from heat; add reserved squash, salt, pepper and 1 cup cheese. Place in buttered casserole and sprinkle with remaining cheese and sprinkle with paprika. Bake at 350 degrees for 30-45 minutes and lightly browned on top.

Kathie's Potato Salad (V)

SUE WOODS

4-6 medium potatoes
4-6 eggs
2 Tbsp dried minced onion, to taste
½ C sweet and spicy French salad dressing
1 C Miracle Whip®
2 Tbsp mustard
Salt and Pepper

Boil potatoes for 30-40 minutes until tender. Run cold water over potatoes for several minutes. Drain and peel potatoes. Cut into bite-size pieces and place in large bowl. Pour French dressing over potatoes; add minced onion to taste and stir gently to coat. Refrigerate for at least one-half hour (several hours is fine also.) Boil 4-6 eggs, cool, peel and chop. Add eggs to potatoes. Salt and pepper to taste. In separate bowl, mix Miracle Whip with mustard. Add dressing mixture to potato and eggs, gently mix all ingredients until coated well. Ready to eat or refrigerate until ready.

Broccoli Casserole (V)

KAREN S. FREEBERSYSER

Butter for greasing casserole dish
2 (10 oz)pkgs frozen broccoli
2 (10 oz) cans cream of mushroom soup
2 C sharp cheese, shredded
1 (2 oz) pkg slivered almonds (optional)
1 individual roll Ritz® crackers, crushed into crumbs
¼ C margarine, melted

Preheat the oven to 350 degrees. Butter a 10 1/2 quart casserole dish and set aside. In a medium saucepan over medium-high heat, boil the broccoli in water to cover for 4-5 minutes. Drain and pat dry. Place half the broccoli on the bottom of the prepared casserole dish. Top with 1 can of the soup, a third of the cheese and half of the almonds. Repeat layers of broccoli, the other can of soup, another third of the cheese and the remaining almonds. Cover with cracker crumbs. Drizzle margarine over the casserole and top with the remaining cheese. Place in the oven and bake until the cheese melts and the top bubbles, about 25 minutes.

Quinoa stuffed peppers (V)

PAT CZOSNYKA

1 medium onion, finely chopped (1 C)
2 Tbsp olive oil
1 rib celery, finely chopped (1/2 C)
1 Tbsp ground cumin
½ tsp cayenne pepper
2 cloves garlic, minced (2 tsps)
1 (10 oz) pkg frozen chopped spinach, thawed and squeezed dry into a towel until all the water is out
2 (15 oz) cans diced tomatoes, drained, liquid reserved
1 (15 oz)can black beans, rinsed and drained
¾ C quinoa
3 large carrots, grated (1½ cups)
2 C grated Jack cheese
½ C blue cheese (or feta or whatever you prefer)
8 large red or other colored bell peppers, halved lengthwise, ribs removed.

Be sure to have all vegetables chopped, and carrots and cheese already grated, as well as spinach thawed and all water is squeezed out before you start cooking, as once everything gets cooking, the recipe goes fast. Also, have canned tomatoes and beans draining while you are chopping the vegetables.

Heat oil in saucepan over medium heat. Add onion and celery, and cook 5 minutes or until soft. Add cumin, cayenne pepper and garlic. Sauté one minute. Stir in spinach and drained tomatoes. Cook 5 minutes or until most of liquid is evaporated. Stir in black beans, quinoa, carrots and 2 cups water. Cover and bring to a boil.

Reduce heat to medium-low and simmer 20 minutes or until quinoa is tender. Stir in half of the jack cheese. Season with salt and pepper. Preheat oven to 350 degrees. Pour liquid from tomatoes in bottom of large baking dish. Fill each half of bell pepper half with mixture, packing in as much as you can, and place in baking dish. Cover with foil and bake 1 hour. Uncover and sprinkle each pepper with 1 tablespoon remaining Jack cheese, then sprinkle with blue cheese. Bake 15 minutes more or until tops of stuffed peppers are browned. For the last 3 minutes, turn on the broiler to get the cheese nicely browned. Let stand 5 minutes. Transfer stuffed peppers to serving plates and drizzle each with pan juices before serving. Any remaining filling can be frozen and used for future stuffed peppers.

Banana Split Fluff Salad

LAVONNE STEVENSON

3.4 oz box instant banana pudding
20 oz can crushed pineapple (do not drain)
8 oz container Cool Whip®
1 C mini marshmallows
½ C walnuts, finely chopped (for inside salad)
2 Tbsp walnuts, finely chopped (for garnish)
½ C mini chocolate chips
2 bananas, sliced
10 oz jar maraschino cherries, halved

Stir together pudding and pineapple until thickened. Fold in Cool Whip. Gently stir in remaining ingredients. Refrigerate at least 1 hour before serving.

Pineapple salad

THE SMITH KITCHEN

1 (3 oz) pkg lime Jell-O®
1 (3 oz) pkg lemon Jell-O®
2 C boiling water
1 C evaporated milk
1 C mayonnaise
1 C crushed pineapple
1 C cottage cheese
Add ½ C or more of pecans, if desired.

Combine lime and lemon Jell-O with boiling water. Let cool, then mix in all remaining ingredients. Once Jell-O is cool, pour into mold. Let set and serve.

Frog-eye Salad (V)

JO OBERG

1 pkg. Acini-De-Pepe® pasta
1 (15 oz) can chunk pineapple or fruit cocktail, drained (save juice)
1 (8 oz) can crushed pineapple, drained (save juice)
2 (11 oz) cans Mandarin oranges, drained (save juice)
1 C sugar
3 eggs
1 Tbsp cornstarch
1 (11 oz.) Cool Whip

Cook macaroni and cool. Cook juice from the canned fruit, sugar, cornstarch and eggs. Cool. Mix with macaroni and fruit. Let stand overnight. Next day add Cool Whip. 🦴

Pickled Beets (V)

KAREN S. FREEBERSYSER

¾ C sugar
¾ C vinegar
¾ C water
1½ tsp salt
1 tsp pepper
1 large onion, thinly sliced
2 (15 oz) cans sliced beets (undrained)
sliced scallions (optional)

In a saucepan, combine the first six ingredients, and bring to a boil. Reduce the heat; cover and simmer for five minutes. Remove from the heat; add the beets. Let stand at room temperature for one hour. Cover and chill six hours or overnight in the fridge. Garnish with scallions when ready to serve. 🦴

FRIENDS DESSSERTS

Honey Spice Bars (V)

MARY WHITEAKER

1 beaten egg
1 C sugar
⅓ C honey
½ C oil
2 C flour
1 tsp baking soda
1 tsp cinnamon
¼ tsp salt
1 C chopped pecans

Mix all ingredients. Press into greased and floured 8" x12" pan. Bake at 350 degrees for about 20 minutes. Spread icing on top while hot from the oven.

Icing
Combine the following ingredients:
1 C powdered sugar
2 Tbsp butter
1 Tbsp water
¼ tsp vanilla

German Chocolate Cake Cookies (V)

PAULA HARDIN

1 German chocolate cake mix
16 oz. cream cheese
½ stick butter
1 tsp vanilla
1 egg
6 oz chocolate chips
1 C chopped walnuts

Mix together first 5 ingredients. Add chocolate chips and nuts. Bake for 10 minutes on wax paper at 350 degrees.

Peugie's Spice Cookie (V)

SALLY B. SIMPSON, STRAY RESCUE VOLUNTEER

¾ C margarine
1 C sugar
1 large egg
½ C mild flavor molasses
2 C flour
Dash salt
2 tsp baking soda
1 tsp ground ginger
1 tsp cinnamon
1 tsp ground cloves

Cream margarine and sugar; add egg and molasses. Add dry ingredients; mix and shape into walnut-sized balls and roll in granulated sugar. Bake for 8 minutes at 375 degrees.

Each time I make this cookie, it reminds me of my own Stray Rescue dog, Peugeot. When he was young, he would get so excited when he realized I was baking this cookie. I would have to watch the cooling racks once I would pull the cookies from the oven for fear Peugeot would jump on the counter to snatch them all. 🦴

Butter Thins (V)

KAREN S. FREEBERSYSER

⅔ C sugar
¾ butter (Imperial®, 1½ sticks)
2 eggs
2 tsp real vanilla
1½ C flour
½ tsp salt

Preheat oven to 350 degrees. Blend sugar and butter. Add 2 eggs, one at a time. Add vanilla. Combine flour and salt. Mix the flour/salt mixture, a little at a time to the sugar/butter mixture until well blended. Drop cookie mixture from teaspoon onto greased cookie sheet. Bake until edges turn brown for about 12 minutes. 🦴

The Ultimate Chocolate Chip Cookie (V)

DAWN NAUGHTON

5 C all-purpose flour
2 tsp baking soda
2 tsp salt
4 sticks butter (not margarine)
1½ cups granulated sugar
1½ cups packed brown sugar
2 tsp vanilla extract
4 large eggs
2 Tbsp water
1 (9 oz) bag caramel-filled milk chocolate morsels
1 (11½ oz) bag semi-sweet chunks
1 (11½ oz) bag dark chocolate morsels
1 C Heath Bits o' Brickle toffee bits

Preheat oven to 375 degrees. Sift together flour, soda and salt; set aside. Beat butter, sugars, vanilla and water in large mixer bowl until creamy. Add eggs, one at a time, beating well after each addition. Gradually beat in dry ingredients until well combined. Stir in the chocolates and toffee bits. Drop by rounded tablespoons full onto parchment-lined cookie sheets. Put the first pan on the bottom rack of the oven and bake for 5 minutes. Then move it to the top rack. Put the next pan on the bottom rack and bake for 6 minutes. Remove the pan on the top rack to cool, move the one on the bottom up to the top, and keep alternating between 5 and 6 minutes each time. (If you have a convection oven, you don't need the rotating trick; just bake as many pans as you can fit in it for 11 minutes.)

This recipe is already doubled, because my philosophy is if I have to clean up the mess anyway, I might as well make twice as many cookies. Makes 6-7 dozen of the best chocolate chip cookies you will ever taste.

Stray Rescue – Judge Smalls

Jan's Famous Butter Cookies (V)

DEBRA MCSTAY

1 C salted butter (2 sticks)
½ C vegetable shortening
1 C sugar
2 eggs
1 tsp vanilla
½ tsp almond flavoring
3½ C flour (all purpose)
⅛ tsp baking soda

Preheat the oven to 325 degrees. Cream butter, shortening, sugar, eggs, vanilla and flavorings together until smooth, then add flour and baking soda. Mix together. The batter will be stiff and can be rolled out for cutting. Bake until done, about 8 minutes or until brown on the bottom. Should make 3-4 dozen. 🦴

Rum Balls (V)

DEBRA MCSTAY

2¼ C vanilla wafer crumbs
1 C finely chopped pecans
½ C rum
1 C powdered sugar
3 Tbsp cocoa
2 Tbsp white Karo syrup

Combine wafer crumbs and pecans. Add all other ingredients. Roll into balls, then coat in powdered sugar or pecans. Makes 40-48 cookies. 🦴

Grandma Helen's Apple Crisp (V)

BECKY SLATIN

3-4 medium apples
¾ C quick cooking oatmeal
¾ C brown sugar
½ C flour
1 tsp cinnamon
½ C butter, softened

Pare apples and slice thin. Arrange sliced in a greased 8" round or square pan. Combine oatmeal, sugar, flour and spices. Cut in butter. Sprinkle mixture over apples. Bake at 350 degrees for 35-40 minutes. Serve warm with cheese wedge, whipped cream or ice cream. 🦴

Carrot Cake (V)

ANGIE HARMON, STRAY RESCUE FOSTER MOM

2 C all purpose flour
2 C sugar
2 tsp baking soda
2 tsp baking powder
2 tsp ground cinnamon
4 large eggs, lightly beaten
1½ C vegetable oil
3 C carrots, grated and peeled
8 oz can crushed pineapple, drained
½ C pecans, chopped

Icing:
1/2 C unsalted butter, room temperature
8 oz cream cheese, room temperature
2 tsp vanilla extract
16 oz box powdered sugar, sifted

Preheat oven to 350 degrees. Grease and flour 3– 8" round cake pans. Sift dry ingredients into a large bowl. Add eggs and oil, and stir until well blended. Fold in the carrots, pineapple and pecans, stirring until thoroughly blended. Pour one-third of the batter into each pan. Bake 30 minutes or until a toothpick inserted in the middle of each cake comes out clean. Cool in pans for 15 minutes. Remove from pans and cool completely on wire racks. To make the icing, combine butter and cream cheese in a bowl, and blend with an electric mixer on medium speed until light and fluffy. Add the vanilla, reduce the speed to low, then gradually beat in powdered sugar until smooth. Frost each layer of cake, stack and frost the whole cake once assembled. 🦴

Uncle Dale's Chess pie (V)

TODD BOHNSACK, LONG TIME VOLUNTEER

3 whole eggs
1½ C sugar
1 Tbsp cornmeal
1 tsp vinegar
1 tsp vanilla
½ C butter
5 Tbsp milk
unbaked pie shell

Measure sugar in mixing bowl add cornmeal and eggs. Beat together, add vanilla, vinegar and milk. Place butter in hot oven until melted. stir into mixture, pour into unbaked pie shell. Bake at 350 for 35 to 45 minutes, or until filling has formed a split in the top 🦴

Sweet Potato Pie (V)

PAM GARTHE, STRAY RESCUE ADOPTER

1 unbaked 9" pie crust
2 C cooked and mashed sweet potatoes (1 lb)
2 Tbsp butter, soften
2 eggs, beaten
1 C white sugar
1 Tbsp all-purpose flour
½ tsp salt
½ C buttermilk
¼ tsp baking soda
1 tsp vanilla extract
Cinnamon, amount to your preference (can change spice, also optional)

Preheat oven to 350 degrees. Mix together mashed sweet potatoes, butter and eggs. In a separate bowl, mix sugar, flour, salt and spice. Add it to sweet potato mix and stir well. In another bowl, mix buttermilk and baking soda. Add it to sweet potato mixture and stir well. Add vanilla extract. Pour filling into pastry shell and bake for 70 minutes until set in center.

Optional pecan topping for 9" pie:
1 C pecans, chopped
½ tsp vanilla extract
1 Tbsp butter, melted
2 Tbsp brown sugar
1 egg
2 Tbsp corn syrup

Mix all ingredients in one bowl. After baking for 45 minutes, take pie out and sprinkle pecan mixture around. Bake for 25 minutes or until center comes out clear when poked.

If you don't want pecan topping, bake for 70 minutes.

Luscious Cheese Cake (V)

DEBBIE CHILDS

56 Ritz® Crackers
6 egg whites
2 C sugar
2 C walnuts, chopped
2 tsp baking powder
8 oz cream cheese, softened
16 oz Cool Whip®
16 oz crushed pineapple, drained

Crush Ritz Crackers in a large bowl. Beat 6 egg whites until very stiff. Add the egg whites, 2 cups sugar, 2 cups chopped walnuts, 2 teaspoons baking powder to the crushed Ritz Crackers. Mix well. Spread this mixture into a 9" x 13" pan and bake in 350 degree oven for 10-15 minutes (crust should be golden,) but not dark. Leave the crust in the pan and cool completely. Whip the cream cheese and fold into Cool Whip. Fold in crushed pineapple to the cream cheese/Cool Whip mixture. Top the thoroughly cooled crust with the cream cheese mixture. Refrigerate till serving time.

Easy Fudge (V)

KATHRYN FLESNER

14 oz can of sweetened condensed milk (Eagle Brand® or generic)
1 pinch salt
1½ bags of favorite chocolate chips (I like to mix dark chocolate, milk chocolate or any favorite chips)
1 tsp vanilla
½ C favorite nuts (pecans, almonds, peanuts)

Heat sweetened condensed milk in microwaveable bowl (2 qt ceramic works best) just until it is hot (approximately 90 seconds.) Do not overcook, as milk can burn. Add chips to hot milk mixture. Stir until chips melt, then add dash of salt and 1 tsp vanilla. Mix well. Add nuts if desired.

Place wax paper in pan. I use a pie tin or a small square pan (8" x 8") and pour mixture into prepared pan. Spread evenly. Allow to cool in fridge. Once set, it is easy to remove the wax paper and place on cutting board and cut into desired pieces.

Bakers Chocolate Chunk Cookies (V)
MICHELLE STREIFF, VOLUNTEER, FOSTER AND ADOPTER

8 oz semi-sweet baking chocolate
½ C butter, soften
½ C brown sugar
½ C granulated sugar
1 large egg
1 C all purpose flour
1 tsp vanilla
1 C oats, quick cooking or process old fashioned
1 tsp baking soda
½ C chopped walnuts or pecans

Preheat oven to 375 degrees. Coarsely chop chocolate. In large bowl, beat butter, sugars, egg and vanilla for 1 minute. Combine flour, oats and baking soda in small ball. Add to butter mixture. Stir in chocolate chunks and nuts. Use small ice cream scoop to drop on parchment lined baking sheet.

Bake 10 minutes. I usually double this and use half chocolate chunks, half semi-sweet chocolate chips. I process the oatmeal until most of flakes are ground, but not as fine as flour though. I usually use walnuts. 🦴

Caramel Apple Crisp (V)
SHAWN BOEDEFELD, VOLUNTEER, DEDICATED TO EMMA LOU AND GIUSEPPE

3 C old fashioned oats
2 C all purpose flour
1½ C packed brown sugar
1 tsp ground cinnamon
1 (10 oz) bag chopped walnuts or pecans (can even use glazed ones)
1 C cold butter, cubed
8 C peeled apples, thinly sliced (Granny Smiths are good)
1 pkg caramel apple wraps
1 C apple cider (cinnamon flavored is good)

Preheat the oven to 350 degrees. Combine the oats, flour, brown sugar and cinnamon in a large bowl. Cut in the butter with knives or a fork until crumbly. Put half this mixture into a greased large foil roasting pan or a 13" x 9" baking dish. Layer half the apples on top of the oat mixture.

Place 2-3 caramel wraps on the apples. Sprinkle half the nuts over the caramels. Put half of the remaining oat mixture over the nuts. Repeat the layers. (The oat mixture will be on the bottom, in the middle and on the top when finished.) Pour ½ cup of the cider over the top. Bake, uncovered, 30 minutes. Pour the other ½ cup of the cider over the top. Bake another 15-20 minutes until the apples are tender. 🦴

Blondies (V)

SHAWN BOEDEFELD, VOLUNTEER, DEDICATED TO SITTER

1 stick unsalted butter, melted
1 C lightly packed dark brown sugar
1 large egg
1½ tsp vanilla extract
1 tsp amaretto
⅛ tsp salt
1 C all-purpose flour
1 C semi-sweet chocolate chips
1 C cinnamon chips
1 C shredded coconut (I use the Mounds® brand)
1 C chopped walnuts or pecans

Heat oven to 350 degrees. Grease an 8" x 8" baking pan. Stir melted butter and brown sugar together in a medium bowl until smooth. Stir in the egg, vanilla, amaretto and salt. Add flour and stir until mixed. Add in chocolate chips, cinnamon chips, nuts and coconut. Spoon the batter into the baking dish and spread evenly. Bake 20-25 minutes until a toothpick inserted into the middle comes out relatively clean. Cool, then cut into squares.

* Any of the extras added—chips, nuts, coconut—can be omitted or replaced with another ingredient of your choice.

Marsha's Chewy Brownie Pie (V)

KAREN GROESSER, VOLUNTEER AND FOSTER PARENT

2 eggs, beaten
1 C sugar
½ C flour
½ C margarine, soften
3 Tbsp cocoa
1 tsp vanilla
¼ tsp salt
½ C nuts

Preheat oven to 350 degrees. Mix all ingredients in a glass pie plate. Bake at 350 degrees for 30 minutes. Garnish with whipped cream, marshmallow cream, nuts or frosting, if desired.

Lemon Pistachio Biscotti (V)

TODD ELLER

4½ all purpose flour
4 tsp baking powder
1 tsp salt
⅓ C brandy
1½ tsp Nielsen-Massey Pure Lemon Extract®*
2 C sugar
16 Tbsp (2 sticks) unsalted butter, softened
4 eggs
1 C shelled pistachios, coarsely chopped and toasted*
2 Tbsp finely grated lemon zest (about 1 lemon)*

Preheat the oven to 350 degrees. Line two large baking sheets with foil or Silpat nonstick baking sheets. Combine the flour, baking powder and salt in a large bowl and mix well. Combine the brandy and lemon extract in a small bowl and mix well. Beat the sugar and butter in a large mixing bowl using an electric mixer until fluffy. Add the eggs one at a time, beating well for each addition. Add the flour mixture alternately with the brandy mixture, beginning and ending with the flour mixture and mixing well after each addition. Add the pistachio and lemon zest; mix well. Divide the dough into four equal portions. Drop spoonfuls of dough from one portion across a baking sheet to form a 2"-wide line with a length of 13". Repeat with the remaining dough portions. Shape the dough into smooth logs. Bake for 35-40 minutes or until golden brown and firm to the touch. Remove from the oven. Cool on the baking sheets on wire racks. Reduce the oven temperature to 300 degrees. Move the logs to a cutting board. Cut on the diagonal in 3/4"-thick slices. Arrange the slices on the baking sheets, cut sides down. Bake for 20-30 minutes or until dry and slightly brown, turning after 10 minutes. Biscotti can be made two weeks ahead and stored in an airtight container at room temperature. Makes 4 dozen.

* For a traditional almond/anise biscotti substitute:
  • Anise extract for the Lemon Extract
  • Toasted almonds for the pistachios
  • Anise seeds for lemon zest

Apple Dumplings (V)

DAWN JASPER (FROM MY GRANDMA HOGG)

2 cans crescent rolls
2 granny smith apples cut, do not peel
1½ C sugar
1 tsp cinnamon
1½ sticks butter, melted
1 (12 oz) can Mountain Dew

Preheat oven to 350 degrees. Grease 9x13 pan. Mix sugar, cinnamon & melted butter.
Roll each piece of apple in crescent roll dough starting at small end of dough. Place rolls in greased 9x13 pan. Pour sugar mixture over rolls. Pour Mountain Dew over rolls. Bake at 350 for 45 minutes. 🦴

Cornflake and Coconut Cookies (V)

TODD ELLER, VOLUNTEER

½ C butter
½ C packed brown sugar
½ C white sugar
1 egg
1 tsp vanilla extract
1 C all purpose flour
1 C cornflakes cereal, crushed
1 C rolled oats
1 tsp baking soda
½ tsp salt
½ tsp baking powder
1⅓ C flaked coconut

Preheat oven 350 degrees. In a large bowl, cream together the butter, brown sugar and white sugar until smooth. Stir in the egg and vanilla. Sift together the flour, baking soda, salt and baking powder; stir into the creamed mixture. Add the oatmeal, crushed cereal and coconut and mix until combined. Drop dough by teaspoonfuls onto a cookie sheet about 2" apart. Bake for 10-12 minutes in the preheated oven. Cookies should be light brown at the edges and on the bottom. Remove from baking sheets and cool on wire racks. 🦴

Apple Enchiladas (V)

JO OBERG

1 (21 oz) can apple pie filling
6 (8") flour tortillas
1 tsp ground cinnamon
½ C butter
½ C white sugar
½ C brown sugar
½ C water

Preheat oven 350 degrees. Spoon one heaping quarter-cup of pie filling evenly down the center of each tortilla. Sprinkle with cinnamon; roll up, tucking in edges and place seam side down in prepared dish. In a medium saucepan over medium heat, combine butter, white sugar, brown sugar and water. Bring to a boil, stirring constantly; reduce heat and simmer 3 minutes. Pour sauce over enchiladas and let stand 45 minutes. Bake in preheated oven 20 minutes, or until golden. Serve with vanilla ice cream.

Snickerdoodles

DAWN JASPER

½ C butter softened
½ C shortening or Crisco®
1½ C sugar
2 eggs
2¼ C flour
2 tsp cream of tartar
1 tsp baking soda
¼ tsp salt

For rolling dough:
2 Tbsp sugar
2 tsp cinnamon
Mix together sugar and cinnamon and set aside.

Preheat oven to 400 degrees. Sift flour, cream of tartar, baking soda and salt. Mix butter, shortening, sugar and eggs. Blend in flour mixture. Roll dough into balls and roll in sugar/cinnamon mixture. Place 2 inches apart on un-greased baking sheet. Bake 8-10 minutes or until set. Immediately remove from baking sheet.

Caramel Puff Corn (aka known as Puff Crack) (V)

DAWN JASPER

1 (8oz) bag Chester's® butter flavored puff corn
1 C butter (do not substitute)
1 C brown sugar
½ C light corn syrup
1 tsp baking soda

Place puff corn in large roaster pan. In 2 quart sauce pan, bring butter, sugar and corn syrup to a boil and cook for 2 minutes. Add baking soda—this will cause the mixture to foam. Stir well and remove from heat. Immediately pour over puff corn in roaster pan and bake in 250 degree oven for 45 minutes, stirring every 10-15 minutes. Remove from oven and spread on wax paper to cool.

Lunchbox Stuffed Dates (V)

CATHY WOOD, COOKBOOK DESIGNER

Use flavorful Medjool or other large dried dates. They are easy to pit and satisfy your sweet tooth.

4 dried dates
1 Tbsp light cream cheese
¼ tsp orange rind, grated
1 Tbsp pecans, chopped

With a small knife cut from one end on one side to the center of the date and remove pit. Combine cream cheese with orange rind and pecans and stuff dates with mixture. Gently press date back together. Wrap in plastic or place in small carrying container for a quick satisfying dessert when you carry your lunch to work or school. Serves one.

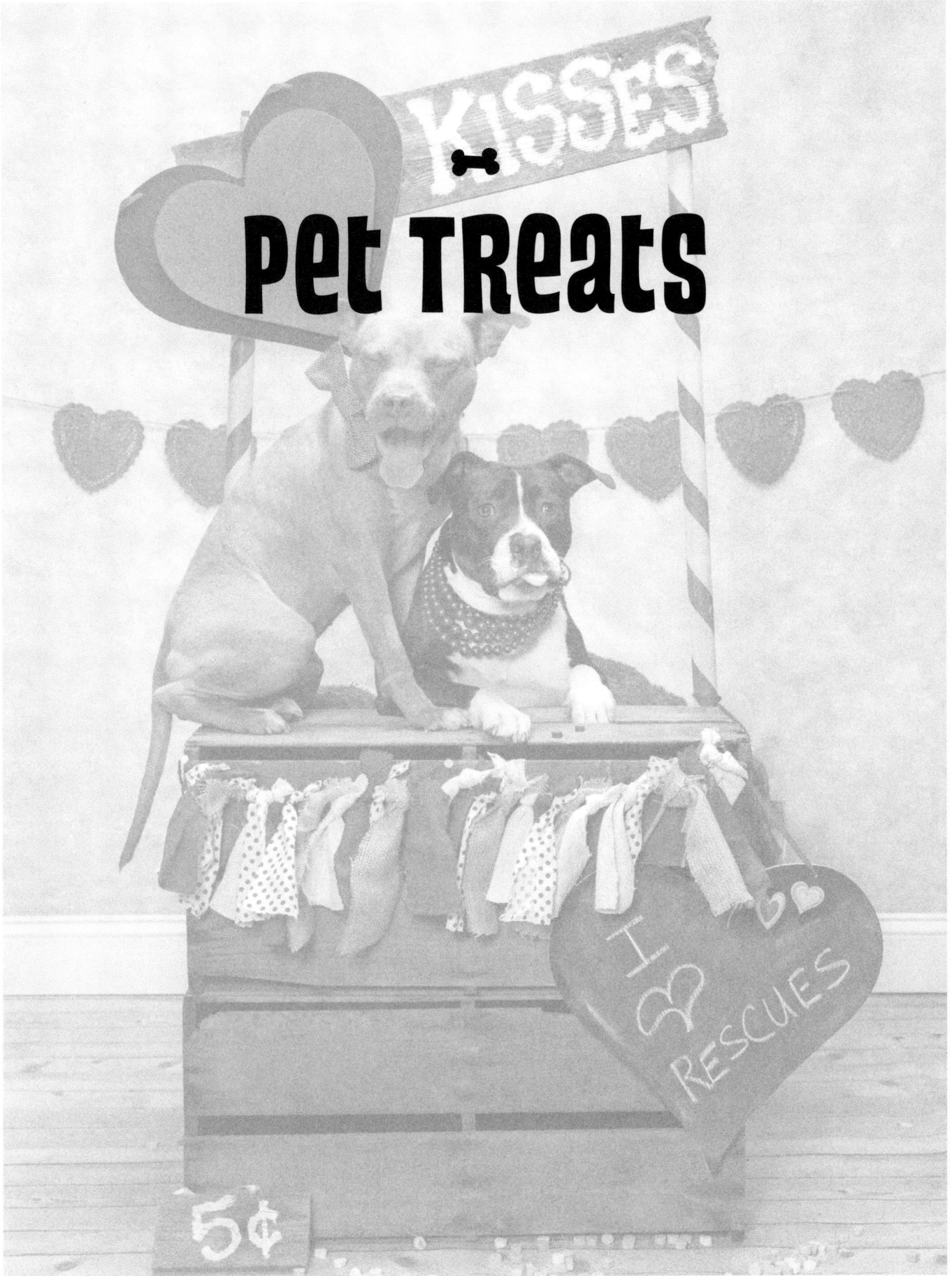

KISSES

PET TREATS

I ♡ RESCUES

5¢

Banana Oat Woofies (V)

Three Dog Bakery, Town and Country, MO

1½ C all purpose flour
¼ tsp baking powder
¾ tsp ground cinnamon
1½ C quick rolled oats
¾ C Canola oil
½ C honey
1 large egg
2 medium – ripe bananas, mashed
1 Tbsp pure vanilla extract

Preheat oven to 400 degrees. Grease 2 baking sheets with nonstick vegetable oil. Stir together flour, baking powder, cinnamon and oats in a bowl and set aside. In a large bowl, using an electric mixer on low speed, mix the oil, honey, egg, bananas and vanilla until thoroughly combined. Stir the dry ingredients into the wet ingredients. Drop the dough by the rounded teaspoonful, 2 inches apart, on the baking sheets. Bake for 12 to 15 minutes or until light golden. Cool to room temperature before serving. Store in an airtight container for up to a week, or wrap well and freeze for up to 2 months.

OP's No-Fat Cookies

RANDY GRIM

1 can of Royal Canin Gastro® Intestinal wet food
¼ C of Royal Canin Gastro® Intestinal dry food
Cooking spray

Place foil on plate and spray with cooking spray. Scoop out tablespoon-size wet food and sort on the plate. Add dry food sprinkles and place in freezer for 2 hours.

OP was shot and is paralyzed, and his digestive system can't handle fat. I always felt guilty giving the other dogs treats and not him, so I had to do so in secret(LOL.) Now he can join the gang at treat time. He loves the crunch of the cookies. This would be great for obese pooches, too.

Jan's Frozen Pup Treats

JAN BLOMEFIELD

1 C plain yogurt
I jar meat baby food

Mix ingredients together until blended. Freeze in mini muffin tins and stick a small dog biscuit as a handle. Can vary by adding mashed banana or peanut butter in place of yogurt; or pumpkin and 1 tablespoon honey.

Oatmeal Peanut Butter Banana Dog Treats (V)

SARAH DENEAU

2 eggs
⅔ C peanut butter
2 C whole wheat flour
1 C cook type oats
1 C mashed banana

Preheat oven to 300 degrees. Combine all ingredients in a mixing bowl. Knead dough and roll out until flattened to desired thickness. Add flour if dough is sticky. Cut out in desired shapes. Line cookie sheet with parchment or lightly grease. Place treats on sheet and bake for 20-25 minutes.

Peanut Butter and Bacon Treats for Dogs

SARAH DENEAU

¼ C bacon drippings
3 Tbsp ground flax seed
¼ tsp sea salt
½ C peanut butter
2½ C whole wheat flour
1 C beef or chicken broth

Preheat oven to 350 degrees. Combine all ingredients with a mixer until combined. Knead dough into a ball. Roll out to ¼" thickness. Add flour if dough is sticky. Use your favorite cookie cutters to cut dough into treat shapes. Place on parchment lined baking sheet and bake 25 minutes, rotating the sheet halfway through. Cool on a wire rack. Store in freezer if you like. You can substitute coconut oil for bacon grease if desired.

Peanut Butter and Pumpkin Dog Treats (V)

SHERRY DENEAU

2½ C whole wheat flour
2 eggs
½ C canned pumpkin
2 Tbsp peanut butter
½ tsp salt
½ tsp cinnamon
Water as needed

Preheat oven to 350 degrees. Mix together the flour, eggs, pumpkin, peanut butter, salt and cinnamon in a bowl. Add water as needed to help make dough workable, but the dough should be dry and stiff. Roll the dough into ½" thick roll and cut into ½" pieces. Bake in preheated oven until hard, about 40 minutes.

Michelle's Pumpkin Pup Biscotti (V)

MICHELLE STREIFF, VOLUNTEER, FOSTER MOM, AND ADOPTER

1 (15 oz) can pumpkin puree
6 Tbsp honey
6 Tbsp water
3 Tbsp canola oil
2 eggs
1½ tsp vanilla extract
3 C whole wheat flour
3 C flour (all purpose)
1½ tsp ground cinnamon
1½ tsp ground ginger
⅓ tsp baking powder
⅓ tsp baking soda

Preheat oven to 350 degrees. In a large bowl, whisk together pumpkin, honey, water, oil, egg and vanilla. In another bowl, whisk together all dry ingredients. Add dry ingredients to wet ingredients, stir until well incorporated, use hands if necessary, as it will be stiff. Transfer to lightly floured surface and knead until dough holds together. Divide into 4 equal pieces, shape each into a log. Place two logs on a parchment lined baking sheet, flatten each log to about 4" wide. Poke holes all over each log with fork. Bake in preheated oven 35-40 minutes or until firm. Place on rack and let cool 30 minutes. Reduce oven temperature to 300 degrees. With sharp knife (I use a bread knife,) cut each log into 1/4-1/2" thick slices. Place cut side down on baking sheet; bake at 300 degrees for 15 minutes, flip each piece over, bake another 15 minutes until hard. Transfer biscotti to wire racks; let cool completely. Store in sealed container 30 days. I freeze them and refill the cookie jar as needed.

Peanut Butter Oatmeal Dog Cookies (V)

MARY THIESSEN

2 C whole wheat flour (you can use another type of flour if your dog is sensitive to wheat)
1 C rolled oats
⅓ C peanut butter, chunky or smooth (I used smooth this time)
1¼ C hot water
Additional flour for rolling

Preheat oven to 350 degrees. Mix dry ingredients together. Mix in the peanut butter and hot water. You may need to add more flour if the dough is too sticky. Knead the dough well. Roll out the dough into 1/4" thickness and cut into shapes with dog cookie cutters. Bake on a lightly greased cookie sheet for 40 minutes. Turn off the oven and let them cool overnight.

Optional: You can make an egg wash if you'd like. Take one egg whisked with a fork and then brushed on with a pastry brush on the treats prior to baking them. Gives them a nice sheen.

KISSES

THANK YOU TO OUR ADVERTISERS

I ♡ RESCUES

5¢

LP Miceli Inc.

3800 Hampton
St. Louis, MO 63109

All lines independent insurance agency

Tina Miceli
314-832-6667 direct
314-802-7607 fax
tmiceli@lpmiceliinc.com

Phycox

Millie

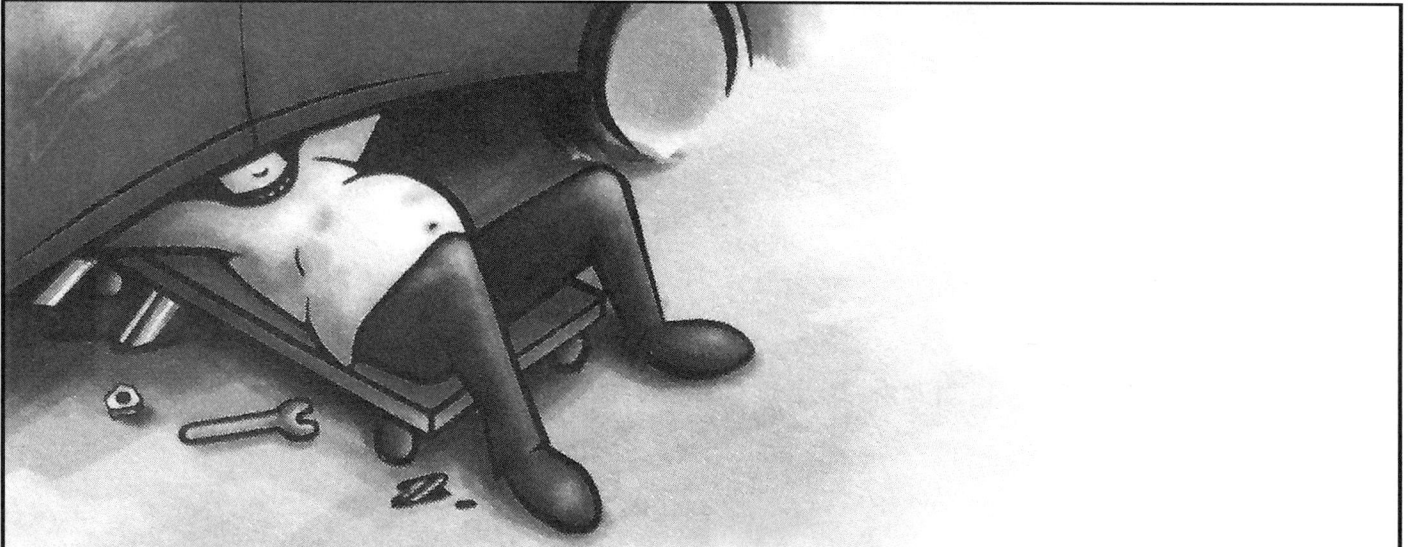

A.M. Clark and Sons, Inc.

7879 Big Bend Blvd.
Webster Groves, MO 63119

314-961-7500

Locally owned and operated • *Like us on Facebook*

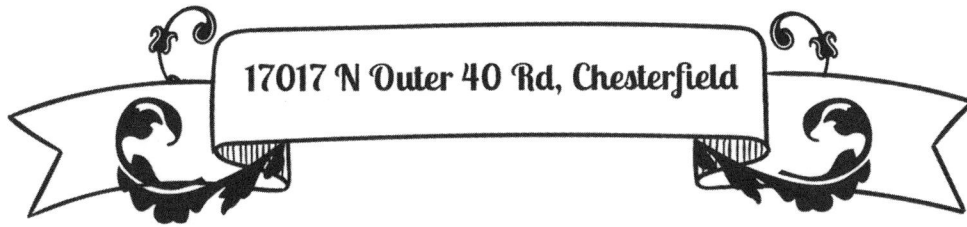

MEASUREMENTS EQUIVALENTS & FOOD SUBSTITUTIONS

MEASUREMENT EQUIVALENTS	
$\frac{1}{16}$ teaspoon	Dash
$\frac{1}{8}$ teaspoon	A pinch
1 tablespoon (tbsp) =	3 teaspoons (tsp)
$\frac{1}{8}$ cup =	2 tablespoons
$\frac{1}{4}$ cup =	4 tablespoons
$\frac{1}{3}$ cup =	5 tablespoons + 1 teaspoon
$\frac{1}{2}$ cup =	8 tablespoons
8 fluid ounces (fl oz) =	1 cup
1 pint (pt) =	2 cups
1 quart (qt) =	2 pints
4 cups =	1 quart
1 gallon (gal) =	4 quarts
16 ounces (oz) =	1 pound (lb)

INGREDIENT	AMOUNT	SUBSTITUTION
Allspice	1 teaspoon	½ teaspoon cinnamon, ¼ teaspoon ginger, and ¼ teaspoon cloves
Baking powder	1 teaspoon	¼ teaspoon baking soda plus ½ teaspoon cream of tartar OR ¼ teaspoon baking soda plus ½ cup buttermilk (decrease liquid in recipe by ½ cup)
Brown sugar	1 cup, packed	1 cup white sugar plus ¼ cup molasses and decrease the liquid in recipe by ¼ cup OR 1 cup white sugar OR 1¼ cups confectioners' sugar
Butter (salted)	1 cup	1 cup margarine OR 1 cup shortening plus ½ teaspoon salt OR ⅞ cup vegetable oil plus ½ teaspoon salt OR ⅞ cup lard plus ½ teaspoon salt
Butter (unsalted)	1 cup	1 cup shortening OR ⅞ cup vegetable oil OR ⅞ cup lard
Buttermilk	1 cup	1 cup yogurt OR 1 tablespoon lemon juice or vinegar plus enough milk to make 1 cup
Cocoa	¼ cup	1 (1-ounce) square unsweetened chocolate
Corn syrup	1 cup	1¼ cup white sugar plus ⅓ cup water OR 1 cup honey OR 1 cup light treacle syrup
Cottage cheese	1 cup	1 cup farmer's cheese OR 1 cup ricotta cheese
Cream (half and half)	1 cup	⅞ cup milk plus 1 tablespoon butter
Cream (heavy)	1 cup	1 cup evaporated milk OR ¾ cup milk plus ⅓ cup butter
Cream cheese	1 cup	1 cup pureed cottage cheese OR 1 cup plain yogurt, strained overnight in a cheesecloth
Cream of tartar	1 teaspoon	2 teaspoons lemon juice or vinegar
Evaporated milk	1 cup	1 cup light cream
Fats for baking	1 cup	1 cup applesauce OR 1 cup fruit puree
Flour–Bread	1 cup	1 cup all-purpose flour plus 1 teaspoon wheat gluten (available at health food stores and some supermarkets)
Flour–Cake	1 cup	1 cup all-purpose flour minus 2 tablespoons
Flour–Self-Rising	1 cup	⅞ cup all-purpose flour plus 1½ teaspoons baking powder and ½ teaspoon of salt
Green onion	½ cup , chopped	½ cup chopped onion OR ½ cup chopped leek OR ½ cup chopped shallots
Honey	1 cup	1¼ cup white sugar plus 1/3 cup water OR 1 cup corn syrup OR 1 cup light treacle syrup
Hot pepper sauce	1 teaspoon	¾ teaspoon cayenne pepper plus 1 teaspoon vinegar
Lard	1 cup	1 cup shortening OR ⅞ cup vegetable oil OR 1 cup butter
Mayonnaise	1 cup	1 cup sour cream OR 1 cup plain yogurt
Molasses	1 cup	Mix ¾ cup brown sugar and 1 teaspoon cream of tartar
Mustard–prepared	1 tablespoon	Mix together 1 tablespoon dried mustard, 1 teaspoon water, 1 teaspoon vinegar and 1 teaspoon sugar
Ricotta	1 cup	1 cup dry cottage cheese OR 1 cup silken tofu
Shallots, chopped	½ cup	½ cup chopped onion, OR ½ cup chopped leek OR ½ cup chopped green onion
Sour cream	1 cup	1 cup plain yogurt OR 1 tablespoon lemon juice or vinegar plus enough cream to make 1 cup OR ¾ cup buttermilk mixed with ⅓ cup butter
Soy sauce	½ cup	¼ cup Worcestershire sauce mixed with 1 tablespoon water
Sweetened condensed milk	1 (14-ounce) can	¾ cup white sugar mixed with ½ cup water and 1⅛ cups dry powdered milk: Bring to a boil and cook, stirring frequently, until thickened, about 20 minutes

STRAY RECIPE NOTES